PRACTICAL
CARP FISHING

PRACTICAL
CARP FISHING

Graham Marsden and Mark Wintle

THE CROWOOD PRESS

First published in 2009 by
The Crowood Press Ltd
Ramsbury, Marlborough
Wiltshire SN8 2HR

www.crowood.com

British Library Cataloguing-in-Publication Data
A catalogue record for this book is available from the British Library.

ISBN 978 1 84797 133 3

Acknowledgements
We would like to thank David and Bridget Keep of Angling Lines and David and Chris Ayres of Sauvellière for hosting our week in France where we endeavoured to complete a number of photographic projects, including a few shots for this book. Similarly, Christchurch Angling Club hosted a day for us with Ian Gemson of Smart Carping at Somerley Lakes. Ian was a great help with his vast array of tackle for some of the photography.

We'd like to thank Quest Baits, Sonu Baits, Kryston, Shimano, Korum, Gardner Tackle and Wychwood for supplying tackle and/or bait.

Adrian Groves helped with some of the photography. Stu Dexter, Chris Yates and Chris Ball helped with a few of the photographs.

Typeset and designed by D & N Publishing
Baydon, Wiltshire.

Printed and bound in Malaysia by Times Offset (M) Sdn. Bhd.

CONTENTS

Preface   6
Introduction   7

1 Getting Started   10
2 About Carp   21
3 Carp Waters and Productive Swims   33
4 Baits   49
5 Tackle: Rods, Reels and Lines   65
6 Other Equipment   77
7 Terminal Tackle and Rigs   93
8 The Method, Hiding the Line and Other Thoughts   109
9 Playing and Landing Carp and Carp Care   121
10 Long-Range Methods   133
11 Surface Fishing   149
12 Long Session Carping in the UK and Abroad   159
13 Winter Carping   167
14 Float Fishing, Stalking and Snag Fishing   173
15 Becoming a Smarter Carper   184

Bibliography   188
Index   190

PREFACE

Many years ago, some time before the 1960s, carp fishing was looked upon as a mystical form of angling that required you to have special powers in order to land your fish. Of course the late and great Dick Walker changed all that by catching the most famous fish in coarse-fishing history, a common carp that weighed 44lb (20kg) and broke the British record. He christened it Clarissa.

Clarissa has a lot to answer for, because she was the fuse that led to the explosion that is carp fishing today, and carp fishing has become *the* most popular branch of coarse angling. From the smaller carp of commercial fisheries to the lone monsters that inhabit secret pools, there are more anglers seeking carp than any other coarse species. Walker would never have believed it: it wasn't at all what he would have imagined on that fateful day in 1952 when Clarissa slipped into the folds of his landing net and began the revolution.

Carp angling has come a long way in the last half century, and during that journey a good number of carp-fishing books have been written, the majority of them aimed at either the raw beginner or the very experienced carp angler. This book aims to slot somewhere in between those two, in that we will not assume that you know nothing about carp fishing, nor will we take it for granted that you have years of experience of carping behind you and want to target extremely difficult-to-catch monsters.

Our objective in this book is to describe and illustrate the wide range of approaches to carp fishing that have been developed over the years. We hope to offer a book that you can read through in one or two sittings, or that you can dip into to refresh your memory of a technique you haven't tried for some time.

We will not neglect the less knowledgeable carp angler, for instance the carper whose only experience is on the usually well stocked small commercial fisheries. He will be introduced to the various approaches he needs to know so that he can branch out into the wider world of bigger fish and bigger waters. Nor will we forget the more experienced carp angler who has already caught some good-sized carp but wants to seek out the bigger fish.

Just as it says on the cover, this book is about practical carp fishing, a comprehensive guide to the various techniques, rigs and baits that are proven and well-established carp-catchers: methods, rigs and baits that are known to work where it matters, on the bank. No bull, just carp.

Graham Marsden

INTRODUCTION

Carp fishing is now bigger than any other type of coarse angling, so much so that it has managed to slide from under the general coarse-fishing blanket and become a branch of angling in its own right. This is quite some feat in view of the fact that over half a century ago carp were considered almost impossible to catch – until the Carp Catchers Club came along, a group of keen anglers led by Richard Walker, who proved that with the right tackle and approach, plus determination, carp could be caught, albeit with difficulty. Nevertheless, carp remained a difficult fish to catch for many years afterwards; especially as most waters either didn't have any carp at all, or were so sparsely stocked it was hard to find any to cast to. Even when you did find a water holding carp, in most cases they were old English strains that seldom exceeded 10lb (4.5kg).

But all that changed over the following decades, because as interest grew in the species an increasing number of waters were stocked with carp, some legally, many otherwise, right up until today when there are more carp in more fisheries than any other species. The post-war housing and building boom created many gravel pits, which, when flooded and allowed to mature, have proved to be ideal carp waters.

It's hard to say whether this beautiful common carp qualifies as an old English strain, but it evokes a traditional vision of carp fishing.

Changeable weather is one factor in carp-fishing success, but perhaps there's a pot of gold at the end of the rainbow?

Big carp like this thirty-five-pounder (15.8kg) caught by Graham have inspired a generation of coarse anglers.

Although the Carp Catchers Club changed the mindset to carp fishing and developed the first specialist carp tackle, there is no doubt that since then there have been further major revolutions in tackle and bait; we will cover these in great detail later in the book. The rigs advocated by the Carp Catchers Club, where weight is kept to a minimum and line allowed to run as freely as possible, are completely contrary to the modern bolt rig. Baits such as boiled potatoes and bread dipped in honey have been replaced with special baits with carefully conceived nutritional values designed to trigger and maintain appetites in carp. But let's not get ahead of ourselves, for you can read all about these tackle and bait innovations in the appropriate chapters.

Although this book isn't meant to be a step-by-step guide, the chapters are presented in a logical sequence, beginning with advice on how to approach carp fishing – there is not much point in knowing a lot about tackle and bait, but little about how to apply it, and no point at all in learning how to apply it if you can't find where to apply it; hence the chapter on locating productive swims.

We should never forget that carp fishing is not a logical sport where a set method and bait will always work. Fish are wild creatures easily affected by the weather conditions, angling pressure and other factors, and no matter how much we think we understand how to catch them, it is vital not to get set in our ways, because even if we crack it on one day, there is always a good chance that the following day will demand different tactics.

This book will teach you about the carp and its habits, the tackle and bait, and the various methods needed to catch them. It will offer practical and down-to-earth advice on what rigs and baits have become established and well proven carp catchers. Furthermore, you will be encouraged to assess each situation as it arises, and advised never to assume that what worked yesterday will work every day. The most accomplished anglers are those who never assume anything, who are open-minded and ever willing to learn.

Quite apart from the tremendous developments in carp fishing itself, the manner in which we develop as anglers has changed enormously in the last fifty years. Long gone are the days of starting with a few tiddler bleak and gudgeon, developing float-fishing skills for roach, perch and dace, maybe progressing to tench, chub and bream, and eventually perhaps pike and carp. The long apprenticeship has gone, and match fishing appeals much less to modern anglers, with an explosion in the availability of carp fishing.

The consequence is that most anglers taking up the sport today will *start* with fishing for carp, rather than aspiring to it. The easy fishing on commercial carp fisheries is an excellent start on the route to becoming a successful carp angler. Practice makes perfect, and even if the carp are on the small side it is good fun to experiment with different approaches; these range from simple float fishing, through basic legering techniques and even some surface fishing with floating baits.

The drawback to such a shortened development as an angler is that you miss out on learning valuable float-fishing, casting and feeding skills that come from years of practice. And such close-range fishing is the best way to get inside the minds of the fish; a clumsy approach will soon scatter the shoal, and getting the feeding

wrong – too much or too little – can be equally devastating.

Comparing roach and chub fishing, say, with carp fishing may seem far-fetched, yet carp are a shoal fish, and just as easily scared, and every bit as demanding of correct feeding and bait presentation. This means that carp fishing demands the same skills in fish location, feeding and bait presentation as other branches of the sport. The added challenge with carp is that they can be more difficult to land due to their size and fighting ability, and are more capable of learning to avoid anglers' baits than most other fish.

Along with the massive increase in the popularity of carp fishing there has been a huge increase in carp tackle. There is a danger here that it is easy to equate having the right gear to having success. In other words, it is easy to *look* like a successful carp angler, which is not the same as *being* a successful carp angler. Some of the most successful carp anglers travel so light it is hard to believe they are carp fishing at all, yet their totally focused approach gets them enviable results. They may only fish for a couple of hours at a time, but they know exactly when, where and how, and that is what puts fish consistently on the unhooking mat.

There are waters where the carp are very big, yet so few and far between that it is only by putting in the hours that success will come. The danger is that understanding whether the approach is the right one becomes nigh on impossible when there is nothing to compare it with. Exponents of this extreme long-stay angling have become known as 'time bandits', which is a little unfair in that those with the time and fanaticism may be the only anglers who stand a chance of catching such huge and elusive carp. In this book, the focus is much more on carp that are catchable by anglers who have to fit their angling around their working and family life, rather than the contrary. And of course, there are those who catch the biggest carp on a regular basis who do not have another life. Don't make the mistake of confusing skilful angling with being a time bandit.

The basic principles of angling are first to find your fish, and then to decide on the best method and bait to catch them. This book covers those principles with regard to the practical aspect of carp fishing.

1 GETTING STARTED

Carp fishing covers a broad spectrum of methods, techniques and approaches, all with one aim in mind: to put carp on the unhooking mat. The carp that anglers target vary from the 'pasties' (small carp) of heavily stocked commercial fisheries, to huge monsters from mysterious waters cloaked in legend. Whilst some anglers dream of landing fifty-pounders from vast lakes, others are content to while away a couple of hours at a quiet club lake catching carp that rarely reach double figures. The tackle, methods and baits – indeed, the entire approach – can be very different, yet they can be equally skilful and satisfying. And in between these two extremes is a multitude of carp methods that form the 'bread and butter' of carp fishing. One of the best things about carp fishing is that there is such a choice of methods we can use to catch them, and there are always new challenges.

If you tire of the more static methods that are often necessary for the most elusive of big carp, there are other, more active ways you can use. You can change from being a cunning 'trapper', who relies on sophisticated baiting campaigns and rigs, to being the active hunter of carp who prefers to find the carp by spotting them, or signs of them, and then uses the most appropriate method and bait according to what he's seen.

The face of modern carp angling in the UK: Mark sets his rods for carp.

The unconventional yet deadly way to catch carp: Graham stalks some big carp that are inches from the bank.

A swim on a typical gravel pit day-ticket water – plenty of room for carp fishing.

With such a spectrum of carp-catching methods and approaches, attempting to pigeonhole each one is foolish. But understanding how the approaches differ, and how to get the best out of each, must be more than useful in becoming a better and more successful carp angler. First of all it is worth exploring just how a great many modern anglers come to carp fishing.

Commercial Fisheries – Easy Small Carp Fishing

There is little doubt that the continuing popularity of commercial day-ticket waters plays a great part in introducing many anglers to carp fishing. The carp may not be very big – some waters have few that weigh more than 5lb (2.3kg) – but there are enough carp in them to make catching them easy, yet provide good sport from hard-fighting fish. The variety of methods and baits that will fool the fish means that sooner rather than later the angler will start catching carp, and it is only natural that once hooked in this way, many anglers feel the urge to catch bigger carp. Even anglers with decades of experience, catching a wide variety of other species and using all sorts of techniques, will, sooner or later, put some time aside for a go at the carp. Carp, quite simply, have become Britain's most popular fish.

Commercial fisheries traditionally offer carp fishing most suitable for the novice and match angler, for the pleasure angler, and for those who are not particularly bothered about catching big fish – and yet that scenario is rapidly proving out of date. From a situation where the carp rarely exceeded double figures it is no longer unusual to fish waters where there are twenty-pounders in realistic numbers, and double-figure fish are commonplace. Of course, this type of carp fishing seems far removed from the conventional view of modern carp fishing. Instead of a multi-rod set-up with bite alarms, boilies and bivvies, the angler on a commercial fishery or club lake could be pole, feeder or float fishing. Yet many of the principles of catching carp are the same, and whatever the approach to carp fishing there is still a need to attract and hold the carp, to fool them into taking the bait, and to land hard-fighting fish. A heavily stocked fishery of this nature makes it much easier to catch the carp, as does the fact that the carp are quite small. And yet it is still those anglers who have best understood the carp's habits that catch the most and the biggest, just the same as with specialist carping.

Certainly this type of fishery offers a means to hone one's skills, albeit on small carp. On some such waters you can watch the carp as they come into the swim, feed, perhaps take the bait, or not, and depart, only to return a few minutes later.

Keep still and you can easily spot carp in clear water.

You can observe the effects of disturbance, of feeding on top of browsing carp, and see how they feed at different depths – although you should always take into consideration that the behaviour of carp in a well stocked commercial fishery, where the fish are almost always hungry, could be quite different from the behaviour of fewer but bigger fish in a water that is rich with natural food.

Apart from the food availability factor, we also have to consider the fact that carp in commercial fisheries will be used to the regular (and often not very careful) tread of big feet around the fishery, so bear in mind that on more difficult fisheries you have to, literally, tread carefully and make sure the carp don't know you're there. Nevertheless, it is through this observation of our quarry that we build up our knowledge, and many of their behavioural patterns can be studied and the knowledge made use of when we move to more difficult waters. To tackle larger carp with little or no experience of smaller samples is rather like expecting to drive a rally car before you've even learned to drive. Lots of practice at feeding, casting and, most importantly, catching carp, will hone the skills needed when you start to push the boundaries to become capable of fishing at longer range for much bigger fish.

It is often the case that carp are found at long range; long casting is one way to catch them.

Stepping Up – More Natural Club Waters

Although one way to gain carp experience at the bottom end is to go to heavily stocked commercial day-ticket venues, many club waters offer similar opportunities. And whereas many commercials are lacking in the sort of features that will expand your fish-locating skills – or watercraft, as it is more commonly known – many club lakes have developed from much older pits, pools and ponds. They are more likely to have features such as sunken trees, reed- and weed-beds, shallow bars and deeper troughs – all ideal features that attract carp yet provide more challenging fishing for the novice carp angler. The stock levels may be much lower, yet there are likely to be enough carp to catch in short day and evening sessions using simple tactics.

With more snags to contend with, and bigger fish too, the lightweight tackle that coped well enough on a snag-free commercial fishery is inadequate, even on a small club lake. It's time to replace the medium feeder rods, light legering rods and poles with heavier tackle – for instance, the gear that would also be appropriate for tench and barbel fishing using rods that used to be known as 'Avon' type. For fish in the 5–10lb (2.3–4.5kg) range on such waters, this will cope better than being totally over-gunned with heavyweight gear better suited to fishing big pits for fish in excess of 25lb (11.3kg). Later, too, the book will cover long-range fishing with very heavy weights, where specialist tackle is required. So the first shift in tackle requirements is underway: matching the tackle to the quarry is vital for all angling.

The approach is changing, too. With quieter banks, much of the time the opportunity arises for some sneakier fishing. It is amazing how close you can get to feeding carp if you tread very softly, wear drab clothing, and don't wave a

Mark caught this 19lb (8.6kg) carp by float fishing, even though float fishing is a generally more accepted method for smaller carp.

flashy rod over their heads. That's assuming you haven't spent ten minutes banging rod rests or bivvy pegs into the ground with a mallet! Incredibly, the carp on many commercial and popular club waters know when the first angler of the day arrives, when there is a match on, when one finishes, and when the last anglers leave for the day. Perhaps that's stretching it slightly, but many anglers advertise their presence so clearly through their heavy-footed, clumsy approach, it is a wonder that they catch anything. For the angler with lots of time on his hands it may be that he isn't bothered about the initial disturbance of setting up camp, baiting the swim and casting out the rigs. But it could be several hours before the carp have settled down, and there is always the chance that there will be further disturbance, in which case the carp never get a chance to settle properly.

It's worth remembering that settled, unwary carp are the ones likely to feed confidently, and confidently feeding carp are catchable carp. Indeed, one of the hazards of popular waters is other anglers. How often do you see two or three anglers fishing together on adjacent swims wandering along to chat with their mates? Their rods

To catch carp very close in you need to sit low and merge into the background.

The bare essentials for carp fishing; the view from the bivvy.

are still doing the fishing and they make little attempt to keep quiet. If one of them does get a run and is away from their rods, then they pound along the bank to get back and hit the run before the line runs off the spool. They are not only decreasing their own chances of fish, but all those in the vicinity too, and perhaps more important, are putting the welfare of the carp at risk. Stealth and quiet are always worth practising, whatever the situation, even when it's totally unnecessary, for they are good habits for any big fish angler to nurture, and the basis of being a good hunter of any wild creature.

At this stage in a carp angler's career his tactics are straightforward, the gear is simple, the rigs unsophisticated and baits are bought over the counter of the local tackle shop. Baiting strategies are often a case of heaving in some samples of whatever everyone else is using, with little thought as to whether a bait has 'blown' or whether the frequency of baiting or the quantity being fed match what is needed. Yet with perseverance, our budding carp angler catches carp. In doing so, he starts to realize that there are many times when the carp are present but not feeding, or feeding but he's not catching them, or he's hooking them but failing to land them; or that the carp's feeding spells occur at certain times of the day or night. There may be long periods of inactivity followed by brief moments of action. It is obvious that a rethink is needed.

Fishing Longer Sessions and for Bigger Carp

It is clear that to fish a short session of perhaps a few hours float fishing or surface fishing with a controller demands total concentration. You must watch the float or controller like a hawk, interpreting every movement, identifying line bites, and nibbles from genuine bites. This concentration is hard work and difficult to maintain beyond five or six hours. Ask any keen match angler just how draining fishing a match can be when having to watch a float for five hours. Overdo it and a splitting headache may result.

Yet this is unlikely to be a factor when carp fishing, for unlike fishing a match, or even pleasure fishing for a few hours when 'fishing for bites' is the norm, larger carp do not bite with anywhere near the same regularity. Most successful carp fishing revolves around knowing a water and the particular habits of the carp that inhabit it, preparation – choosing the swim, baiting it, and presenting a hookbait – and then waiting for things to happen. If you make the waiting aspect as comfortable as possible then you can fish for many more hours, even several days and nights should you wish.

Once that preparation is done and the waiting game takes over, the carp angler just needs a means of fishing these much longer sessions in a relaxed manner. He doesn't want to be perched upright on a fishing box holding the rod. He wants to be able to cover more of the swim by using two or more rods, and to be alerted to a run when it happens. The set-up for doing so is what most anglers think of when carp fishing is mentioned. Two or three rods set up on a rod-pod with bite alarms, and the angler relaxing in a bivvy on a bedchair. To survive long sessions means planning for meals, for having enough bait for the extended session and, most important, understanding why choosing a swim becomes more vital than ever if you are proposing to stay in it for a long session. Fishing a long session does not preclude moving on to a new swim when conditions change, but when you've got enough kit to set up an Everest base camp, moving is a laborious task, and few long-stay carp anglers are prepared to do it.

Whereas the short session angler can take a chance on a swim, travel light, and maybe fish a relatively easy water, following such an approach for the longer haul angler is likely to lead to many blank sessions. Arguing that the fish are really much harder to catch is not a valid argument when truly effective anglers turn up on the same water and catch big fish, sometimes within minutes. Much of angling is simple when it is broken down into the constituent parts, and carp fishing is no different.

On the majority of waters that hold carp, including big ones, some of them can be caught at short range: not all of them, but some of them. In fact, on many carp fisheries the margins can be the best place to catch the bigger carp, as margin patrolling is one of their habits. The basis for successful margin fishing is, however, stealth and silence: it is not an approach for the noisy, fidgety angler. But there's more on this in a later chapter.

The consistent success of many carp anglers is often put down to them having a 'secret' bait, but such things exist more in the minds of anglers who want to believe in them and who do not put in the research and hard work prior to venturing on to a water. The only 'secret' there is to successful fishing, for any species, is knowledge of the fish's feeding habits, the ability to choose a swim where the fish will feed in a given set of conditions, and offering them a bait they can't refuse. More 'codfather' than 'godfather', but the principle is the same.

It's the same with rigs. There is nothing magical about them, and the best ones do a simple job without any complications. They present a bait without arousing the carp's suspicions and hook the fish efficiently when it takes the bait into its mouth. There are some excellent rigs that have been devised by carp anglers, and there are some weird, overcomplicated ones that were devised more to please the angler than to fool the fish. Rigs are important, of that there is no doubt, but clear thinking and simplicity on rigs is going to be a better bet in the long run than attempting to devise ever more complex ones simply for the sake of it.

Feeding a swim has new dimensions, too. Several hungry carp or a shoal of bream can clean a swim of bait in a matter of minutes. You could be unaware that this has even happened, or be lazy in topping up the swim. Feeding a swim causes disturbance – how much depends on the range and type of feeding, yet the opposite approach of depositing a mountain of bait into a swim in the vain hope that it must surely suffice can be equally misguided. There's little point in filling up the carp if it leads to them moving out of the swim to rest up and digest the heavy meal.

The techniques of feeding also change, from the simplest – introducing a few free samples of bait by hand, catapult or throwing stick – to the more sophisticated techniques utilizing PVA bags, spods and even baitboats. There is a fine balance between feeding a swim with a generous amount and leaving it undisturbed, and feeding little and often, which means disturbing the swim regularly. You must find the balance between the two that keeps the swim topped up with feed, but does not rely on one big helping that could overfeed most of the carp that visit the

RIGHT: Keep quiet enough, and carp will come this close.

*BELOW: A classic shot of Redmire Pool.
(Courtesy Chris Ball)*

swim. In marginal and close-in swims, loose feeding much reduces the possibility of disturbance. Understanding what baits can hold and attract carp into a swim is vital, and equally important is deciding just how much of that particular bait to introduce, and how often, for some baits are far more filling than others.

Similarly a rethink is required on tackle. Whilst a light carp rod or even adapted barbel gear is fine for short-range fishing for carp to 10lb (4.5kg), it is severely limited for fishing at longer range and for tackling bigger carp. That means heavier carp rods designed for the job, with reels and lines to match. Like most fishing it is a case of using the tackle best suited to the job. It also means thinking about landing nets, unhooking mats, hooks and rigs.

This change in approach means that it is vital to know which venues actually contain bigger carp that are catchable. It is no use hoping your local one-acre pond will produce good numbers of 20lb (9kg) carp, with the possibility of a thirty-pounder if the reality is that the biggest fish is 12lb (5.5kg). It pays to do your homework, the essential research into any potential venues. But make sure you ask the right people, and don't take the word of the local optimist who has arms with a wider reach than the M1 motorway and scales to match. Ask a number of people, especially the locals who fish there, and then reach a realistic conclusion.

Some very small waters contain some very big carp, so don't let the size of some waters put you off. There is a growing trend to develop small waters of 2 to 4 acres (0.8 to 1.6ha) just for specimen carp fishing, and this will transform the sport in this respect. These special waters may have no carp less than around 10lb (4.5kg) within them, and the biggest will top out at 30lb (13.6kg) or even 40lb (18kg), with the potential for even bigger fish. It's worth bearing in mind that Redmire Pool, the water that produced Dick Walker's 44lb (20kg) record carp and Chris Yates's 51lb 8oz (23.4kg) carp that became the new record, plus numerous other big carp, is less than 3 acres (1.2ha) in size.

A more likely venue for bigger carp these days is a flooded gravel pit that has been developed as a carp fishery. As these waters mature, a process that takes decades, the formerly bare banks become wooded, silt beds develop and the carp stocks mature. For such waters, often available via club book, day ticket or syndicate, it is vital to find out what is in the water. Out-of-date or speculative information may be worse than useless. One good example that comes to mind is of a Hampshire pit of 8 acres (3.2ha), first stocked with carp in the early nineties. After a decade, the carp bred and grew well, with plenty of doubles and a sprinkling of twenties. A stocking exercise in 2003 that was supposed to boost big roach and rudd stocks by netting a nearby lake turned up a good number of carp to 28lb (12.6kg), and, despite there being no need to boost the already prolific carp stocks, these were introduced.

Thus on the face of it you have a prolific lake with carp to 28lb, but what you only find out through much searching is that there was a significant fish kill in the spring of 2005 when at least 200 sizeable carp died. The water is now far from prolific as far as carp are concerned, although it still produces a few. It is continuing to recover because the introduced carp have bred successfully, but it will be some years before it is anything like as good as it was in 2004.

Similarly, many waters gain a reputation for producing numbers of big fish – say, over 30lb (13.6kg) – when the reality is that the same handful of big ones is caught over and over again. This is where the hard work starts. You need to sort the wheat from the chaff, the consistently productive water from the one that is so hard that you could spend years from your life just trying.

The Busy Man's Approach to Big Carp

The pace of modern life, and the multitude of demands on an angler's time as regards work and family, mean that for many it is a case of fitting in what they can, when they can. Apart from a handful of occasions each year, long sessions are out of the question. Instead, the carp angler becomes an opportunist. He figures where, when and how to catch good-sized, even big carp in sessions that could be as short as an hour or two. The multi-rod, bivvied-up approach

Eddie Cardus with a superb 26lb (11.7kg) summer carp.

is too slow for these short sessions. This means sneaking up on the carp in the margins, amongst the snags and in the quiet, out-of-the-way places. It may mean using conventional float-fishing tactics, again close in, or fishing for the carp using surface bait methods. The gear is still broadly mainstream carp tackle, although the big pit gear is less useful. By carrying a minimum of gear, the angler can be in position and fishing quickly with a minimum of fuss in just a few minutes. Part of the session might be dedicated to carefully feeding up the swim to get the already present carp competing for the bait. Then one careful cast … The opportunist carp angler may settle for a single fish – job done, and steal away before his presence has even been noticed.

Some keen carp anglers try to squeeze in some longer sessions without interrupting work and family life, very often putting in a few hours carping in the mornings, straight from a night shift, or in the evening, fishing to the early hours of the morning following a day shift. Others of a more determined (or dafter) nature will fish through the night and go to work the following morning, although they're sensible enough to choose a water where runs are few and far between and can therefore sleep for most of the night undisturbed.

The key, as always, is to choose your venues according to the time you have available. Select easier venues for those opportunist sessions when you have only an hour or two to spare, and harder waters for longer sessions, and for those times when you just have to work and fish almost at the same time and need to sleep for much of the time when your bait lies in the water. The latter is, of course, a desperate plan, but if you have no choice then it is one you could try occasionally to see how it turns out.

So Many Approaches, So Little Time …

Amongst these approaches there is a right one for any carp angler seeking to improve his carp-catching skills, and there's no reason why you shouldn't vary your approach when the mood takes you. Too many tough sessions in a row with little to show for it can be demoralizing, and a couple of easy sessions on a fish-packed commercial or at least an easy water will put a bend back in your rod, remind you to have some fun, and recharge your batteries.

RIGHT: *Ian Gemson carp fishing; the bait is in, the rods are out, time to get comfortable and watch and wait.*

BELOW: *Mark keeps low to avoid scaring a big carp.*

On the other hand, flitting between lots of different approaches can be confusing. Successful carp angling certainly involves what was once described as controlled impatience. That means thinking about your fishing when you are fishing, scanning the water for signs of moving or feeding fish, and even thinking laterally to create more carp-catching opportunities. Certainly make the most of the time you have available, but always have some time for a simple, relaxing carp-fishing session when you can lie back and think of nothing at all …

First and foremost, fishing should be fun.

2 ABOUT CARP

Carp have been the most studied coarse fish of the modern era, and there is little about them that we don't know. Yet the big question is, just how extensive does your knowledge of carp need to be for you to become a better carp angler? It would be possible to write an entire book just about the natural history of carp, yet this wouldn't necessarily help you catch more or bigger fish of the species, and it would hardly be the 'practical guide' that this book aims to be. Nevertheless, there is no doubt that some knowledge is useful, and you can learn much from quiet observation of

carp in their natural habitat. In addition, getting to know the effects of the weather and the seasonal variations on the carp's behaviour can all help you plan your carp fishing more profitably.

Therefore a basic study of the carp and its feeding habits can never be a bad thing, because the more you know about the fish you are trying to catch, the better are your chances of devising a plan that is right for your water, the time of year and the time of day or night that you are fishing – and this all helps to ensure that you are fishing in the right spot.

Simply massive – the world record common carp.

Varieties of Carp

Worldwide there are many species of carp, although in the UK the angler is only likely to encounter three of them, and this book is principally concerned with just one – commonly known as the king carp. The two other species of carp, with which this book is not concerned, are the crucian carp and the grass carp. Carp tactics as described in this book will work for the grass carp (they can reach weights of around 40lb/18kg in the UK), although their habits differ somewhat from king carp. The crucian carp, like its similar cousin the goldfish, rarely exceeds 3lb (1.4kg), and is most often sought with light float tackle, with which this book is not concerned.

To further confuse things we have the wild carp, or 'wildie' as anglers affectionately call it. The wildie is the closest in shape and characteristics to the original carp stocked in stew ponds by the monks in the Middle Ages, although relatively few wildies remain in this country. It is a fact though, that some common carp are often identified as wildies simply because they have the wildie's characteristic long, lean shape, probably caused either by old age or poor diet. Furthermore, they generally only reach a maximum of not much over 10lb (4.5kg).

ABOVE: *Grass carp can reach more than 40lb (18kg) and often fall to carp tactics, especially floating baits.*

LEFT: *A carp by name, but you'll have to read Mark and Graham's book on pole fishing for advice on catching crucian carp.*

Long, lean common carp like this one are often called 'wild' carp, but whether true wild carp still exist is open to debate.

Some writers have expressed doubts about the continuing existence of the so-called wildies. Their argument is that there have been so many stockings in the last fifty years that the continuing survival of this strain without breeding with the much more common 'king' carp is extremely unlikely. Yet in some long forgotten, reedy pool there are no doubt a few survivors of this strain. If you are lucky enough to stumble upon such a venue, you may well be rewarded with memorable old-style carp fishing. What the carp lack in size they make up for in fighting ability, and if you can scale down the tackle to suit the conditions, perhaps using a light carp, a barbel or even an Avon rod, with 8lb line, you can have explosive carp fishing, as the wildie lives up to its name and charges off with an unbelievable rate of acceleration.

Graham has caught wildies in a small pool that was no more than a foot deep with water that lay over three feet of silt, but the wildies he caught to around 8lb (3.6kg) were like golden bullets that shot from one side of the pool to the other in one mad, sudden and incredible burst of speed that caused wisps of smoke to curl up from the drag of the reel.

The three varieties that concern us are variations of the king carp; they are known as the

Mirror carp have many variations on scaling, with fully scaled mirrors being the rarest – here's a more common variation.

common, the mirror and the leather carp. The common carp is fully scaled, similar to most other species of coarse fish; the mirror has large scales in irregular patterns that vary from one fish to another, with some having just a few very large scales and another rather beautiful variety of the mirror being fully scaled. Leather carp have virtually no scales except perhaps for a few close to the dorsal fin or the wrist of the tail. There is another, less common variety, known as the linear, which has a single row of scales along the lateral line. On modern carp waters in the UK, however, it is most likely you will be fishing for a stock that consists of a mixture of mainly common and mirror carp, with a few leathers and possibly one or two linears, although there will be waters where any one of the varieties will be dominant. In any case, the stock will have been selected for their fast-growing characteristics and will be capable of reaching 20lb (9kg), 30lb (14kg), even 40lb (18kg) and more, and certainly way beyond that achievable by those native 'wildies' stocked in the middle ages.

Before we leave carp variants it is worth noting that you will occasionally come across koi carp ('koi' being Japanese for carp, with the homophone being love or affection), which are a coloured strain of carp, a cultivation of the common carp, that have been specially bred in eastern Asia. The best examples are worth many thousands of pounds to enthusiasts who stock their ponds with them. Less popular variants,

often crossed with our more familiar naturally coloured carp, have become more widespread in the UK in the past twenty years. Colorations known as 'metallics' and 'ghost' are found in some waters. It is noticeable that the koi variants tend not to reach the sizes of the other king carp with twenty-pounders being the exception, and a maximum of around 10lb to 15lb (4.5kg to 7kg) being more common. The best known of the koi variants is the ghost carp, or ghostie, as it is most commonly called.

How 'Intelligent' are Carp?

Let's first define what we mean by 'intelligence' when we're referring to fish. Even the scientific community is divided when it comes down to defining intelligence where we mortals are concerned, but for the sake of this deliberation let's say that intelligence is the ability to think with a purpose and solve problems. So in that respect carp, probably like all fish (as far as we know), are not intelligent at all. So what we are left with is instinct; that built-in ability to recognize and react to feeding triggers, spawning urges and, of course, danger. However, to make it as easy as possible for the reader to follow the gist of this chapter, we will continue to refer to this instinctive behaviour as intelligence.

Carp are amongst the most intelligent of fish, so it is little wonder that their infuriating ability to avoid capture at times frustrates our efforts. On the other hand, at times their greed can make them relatively simple to catch, and turns many a well worn theory on its head. There is no doubt that carp are a fish species that responds to being educated, or trained – so they learn that the carp angler's richly nutritious but unnatural food is good for them, but that it can also be dangerous in that sometimes when they eat it they find themselves resisting a trip to a landing net. It is this constant challenge to find new baits, rigs and methods and to stay one step ahead of the carp that carp anglers find so fascinating.

Part of this superior intelligence in carp possibly derives from their sheer size; a big carp of 30lb (14kg) or more has much more space for a brain than a tiny gudgeon or minnow. In addition, carp have other advantages when attempting to avoid

Koi carp are a specially bred variety of common carp.

capture – for example their sheer bulk and strength, which enables them to provide a heart-stopping fight when on the end of a line. As will be described later in the book, correct tackle selection is essential, given the carp's renowned fighting ability. But the carp's intelligence is also a driving factor in our attempts as anglers to outwit them. Their seeming ability to detect our sometimes crude attempts to fool them can make for frustrating times, yet the tremendous array of baits and tackle available, and our collective knowledge of rigs and methods, and especially the carp's behaviour in different conditions, make this problem far from insurmountable.

One of carp fishing's heart-stopping moments: a carp approaches a floating bait.

The Catchability of Carp

Bigger carp can be extremely hard to catch at the best of times, but especially when they have been spooked by disturbance. Sometimes it is hard to avoid all disturbance, for despite our best efforts, other factors such as wildfowl or, more likely, other anglers, spoil our chances for a while. In time the carp will settle and regain confidence, but there is little doubt that spooked carp are much harder to catch than those that remain unaware of our presence.

There are times when we can see the carp approach our bait, either when surface fishing or when looking from cover into clear water. We know that the carp are unaware of our presence, yet they are wary of the one bait that has a line and hook attached. This is particularly true when presenting a floating bait. Educated carp approach the bait with great caution; they knock it about, or even come up beneath it, testing the water all around the bait by encircling it with an open mouth. Their refusal to actually take the bait is unbelievably frustrating, and furthermore they seem to transmit their own caution to other carp in the vicinity.

What often works against carp is their greed. In many instances it is possible to feed the carp in such a way that they are not made wary. This art of feeding means much more than just dumping a pile of bait into the swim and hoping: rather, it means understanding what is happening in the swim, so that in time – and not necessarily a long time, maybe even a matter of minutes rather than hours – it is possible to get the carp competing for food, rather than picking and choosing which baits to take. In instances like this their guard is relaxed, making this the angling equivalent of a confidence trick. Take this a step further and be selective as to which carp you present your bait to, and you might just select one of the elusive big ones that usually let the smaller fish take the bait.

Through tagging experiments there have been surprising results on the catchability of carp. One would expect all carp to be equally catchable, with perhaps the smaller carp being easier to catch than bigger ones. What transpires is that the carp population splits into very rough thirds. About a third of carp are easy to catch, and these fish are caught very regularly. The next third are caught much less frequently, and may appear to adopt different feeding strategies, albeit subconsciously. They may only feed confidently when the lake is practically deserted, or only near snags. They may have found a quiet, hardly fished part of the lake that offers sufficient natural food to avoid reliance on the more abundant anglers' baits. Whatever their mode of avoiding capture, they will be much more challenging than the first group.

Finally we have the remainder, the final third, which appear never to get caught. It was suggested by one lake owner that all that needed to be done was to identify and remove those impossible fish! If only it were so easy!

But let's not forget the mug fish: the carp that, on some heavily fished waters, is caught almost every day – there is usually at least one in every water. It is often easily recognizable through some deformity or, if it's a mirror, by its unique scale pattern; it usually has a pet name, and anglers return it gently to the water with a farewell message along the lines of, 'See you again soon, me old mate!' We don't know *why* any particular mug fish is a mug, unless, of course it has some deformity of the mouth that prevents it from conventional feeding. They're usually no different in general appearance to any other carp, but for some reason they just haven't got that instinctive edge that other carp have of recognizing danger. We have all heard the old wives' tale of someone having the memory of a goldfish, and in the case of the mug fish it may be that they have the piscatorial equivalent of dementia, with forgetfulness even worse than that of a goldfish!

How Long Do Carp Live?

It is generally thought that carp grow for around fifteen or sixteen years on average. Once they

Chris Yates set the carp world alight back in 1980 when he broke the long-standing record held by Dick Walker. (Courtesy of Chris Yates)

reach their maximum length their weight can increase further, by becoming fatter and increasing their girth, or it can then fluctuate around a certain weight over the years depending on conditions and, it must be said, just how much of the modern carp anglers' high nutritive value (HNV) baits they consume. After a long cold winter, especially on those waters that are not popular for winter carping, their weight could drop, whereas an especially mild winter followed by a long hot summer could see a carp's weight hit a peak.

How long a carp lives beyond the fifteen year average is difficult to say with any degree of certainty, and there must be a considerable variation from fish to fish and water to water. There is evidence, however, of carp living for more than double the fifteen years, a good example of this being the previous record fish known as 'The Bishop' that Chris Yates caught from Redmire Pool back in 1980 at 51lb 8oz (23.4kg). Records of its various captures (identifiable by its unique scale pattern) exist from the fifties onwards, and this led to being able to establish its age.

What has been discovered is that selective breeding to achieve especially fast-growing carp can lead to a strain of carp that seem to grow fast but die young. The opposite applies, too, in that some slow-growing old strains seem to live forever, the only clue to their great age being that in time their coloration gradually darkens.

What Factors Affect Their Growth?

A number of factors affect the growth of carp. These include the richness of the water and the availability of both natural food and that thrown in by anglers, the stocking density, the strain of carp, and the prevailing climate. Let's take a look at each.

What do we mean by the 'richness' of the water? Without delving into technical detail, the richness of a water is a reference to its ability to sustain fish in a healthy environment where they can thrive, successfully spawn (without spawning too successfully) and grow. The carp may only spawn successfully in bigger waters in exceptionally hot summers, whereas in some waters they will spawn more than once.

The availability of natural food, the bloodworm (mosquito larvae), water snails, insect larvae, water fleas (daphnia), crustaceans and other

ABOVE: This 19-acre (7.6ha) Hampshire pit is a typical modern big carp venue.

The high back and deep belly of this mid-thirty held by Graham is typical of modern varieties of carp.

creatures that make up the bulk of a fish's natural diet should be such that it provides more than enough for the carp to increase its weight conversant with, or beyond, the growth of its skeleton, and then to continue to maintain that weight, or ideally, from an angler's point of view, increase its bulk when skeletal growth has finished. The growth rate of carp can be accelerated on popular carp waters where carp anglers are continually introducing modern highly nutritious baits; in the main pellets and boilies designed to trigger the appetites of carp and provide a diet that encourages vigorous growth. It is thought that on some heavily fished waters anglers' baits can provide more than 70 per cent of the carp's diet.

The stocking density affects the growth rate in that the more mouths there are to feed, the less food there is to go round, and the more effort is needed by the fish to find it. Not just carp, but other fish, especially bream and tench, will want to plunder any available larder, natural or otherwise, and this will affect the growth rate. Put simply, however, the biggest fish are usually found in waters where the stock density is very low, and the fish have to put in little effort to find it. The flip side is the modern commercial fishery that is usually excessively overstocked to keep the fish hungry, where they have to be continually looking for food just to maintain life, let alone growth, and therefore provide anglers with a steady stream of bites even in the most adverse conditions. Some strains of carp have been bred to grow quickly, somewhat beyond the growth rate of the normal run of fish, given sufficient food of the right quality.

The Effects of Temperature on Carp

How does temperature affect carp? All fish are cold-blooded, and therefore their behaviour is affected by water temperature. Fish live in waters that vary from barely above freezing to bordering on lukewarm, so where do carp fit into the overall picture? After all, at one end of the spectrum you have true cold-water fish such as grayling, and at the other end fish such as cichlids that we commonly call tropical fish. One is a remnant of the ice ages thriving in cold water that is less than 10°C (50°F), and the other needs water of 26°C (80°F) and above to survive.

If we think of where the carp evolved and originated, the area around the Caspian Sea, it is clear that the carp is neither suited to sub-arctic nor equatorial conditions. Hot summers and moderate winters – a Mediterranean climate – approximates to the carp's ideal. That is warmer than the climate of southern Britain, and indicates that as one moves north, the conditions, as far as temperature is concerned, are likely to become less favourable. That is a generalization, of course. Closeness to the sea, altitude, the characteristics of the carp water and local weather variations mean that there are cold waters in the south and warm suntraps in the north. On the whole, however, the temperature gradient has a discernible impact on the carp-fishing potential.

For carp to thrive it needs to be sufficiently warm for them to spawn successfully, at least some of the time. When water temperatures are sustained at 17–20°C (63–68°F), the carp are able to develop the roe for spawning. Spawning occurs in late spring and early summer; sometimes it is very early, such as in 2007 when the exceptionally sustained warm weather in April triggered spawning across Britain before the end of the month. A prolonged cold spring can delay spawning to as late as early July. Some years there are topsy-turvy conditions, where brief warm spells that start to trigger spawning are interspersed with cold snaps. In such conditions, the carp may fail to spawn successfully at all in many waters, and there is a danger of spawn-bound fish. In some deep and shaded cold lakes, spawning may virtually never take place, with the carp stock of the water only sustained by stocking. In much warmer climes, the carp can spawn more than once during the course of some summers.

If you are planning carp trips during late spring and early summer it is worth taking note of this spawning trigger. There is little worse than arriving at a water to find the carp totally preoccupied with spawning, and no realistic chance of sport for a week or two at best. That does not mean that you cannot catch the carp, but given the debatable legal and ethical aspects, the carp are best left alone anyway, until they have recovered from their exertions.

This 30lb-plus (13.6kg) mirror caught by Mark in early May shows signs of developing spawn. Another three weeks and, given the right weather conditions, it is unlikely to be feeding.

The warmer months, therefore, are when the carp are most active. If the water temperature gets too high, the carp may stop feeding altogether. In such conditions, the carp angler will need to fish when the conditions cool down, rather than during the heat of the day. The 2003 heatwave provided a good example of this. Mark fished a shallow gravel pit using floating baits during August 2003. Until 7pm, the carp showed little interest, although the proximity of the water to the sea (4 miles away) meant that there was some sea breeze but not enough to cool the water to encourage the carp to feed. Yet as soon as the water cooled a little the carp fed avidly.

Prolonged heatwaves, especially on the continent, may put paid to good carp fishing until conditions freshen and cool. This is one of the few instances where falling water temperatures are likely to be beneficial to your chances. When water temperatures are in more normal summer ranges – 15 to 20°C (59–68°F) – a sudden and significant drop in water temperature can wreck your chances, at least until the carp acclimatize.

The Effects of Cold Temperatures

In winter, temperature can be even more critical. Above around 10°C (50°F) your chances remain reasonably good; below it they diminish, yet there is an unpredictability that sometimes defies belief. For complex reasons it is sometimes possible to make good catches of carp from semi-frozen lakes, ones that are substantially cooler than 10°C. It may be that the carp are triggered into feeding through sheer hunger, slight rises in temperature, or there may be parts of the water where underground springs bring warmer water into the lake.

At lower temperatures the carp's metabolism – the speed at which it can digest food – is much slower. Feeding spells, when they do occur, will be brief, and once sated the carp may not feed for many hours. It may be that they will only feed during the part of the winter day when water temperatures are at their highest, which is likely to be mid-afternoon. Winter prospects are likely to be at their best when the prevailing wind is south to south-west, brisk to strong, and warm. The water movement and rising temperatures may well wake the carp from their slumbers.

You also have to look at the food chain, for not only does temperature affect the carp, it also affects the natural food upon which they feed. When the temperature plummets, the natural food ceases to thrive and decreases drastically, with different temperature levels affecting different types of natural food.

But that is all without taking into account the 'angling factor', by which we mean the influence that angling has on the carp's feeding behaviour, regardless of (to some extent, anyhow) the water temperature. It has become increasingly obvious over the years that the most productive winter carp waters are the most popular ones, in that a constant supply of anglers' baits keeps the carp rooting for food. In the early days we viewed this the 'wrong way round', in that we assumed that some waters were popular in winter due to the carp feeding well in that season. Then it became apparent that in many cases it was the fact that anglers were still fishing through winter that kept the carp feeding with some regularity. On those waters where anglers more or less gave up fishing through winter, the carp, unable to find the boilies, pellets and particles that they were used to finding and feeding on in the warmer months, drifted into a type of semi-hibernation where they simply stopped looking for food. Those few anglers who may have continued fishing these same waters, and fed sparingly, knowing that the carp were not inclined to feed, suffered the consequences and caught little.

Those of you with fish ponds in your garden can quite easily test this conjecture yourself. For one winter do not feed the fish regularly and observe their behaviour when you introduce the odd morsel of food. It is almost certain the fish will largely ignore it. Then in another winter continue to feed them regularly – though obviously not with anywhere near the same amount of food you would use in the summer months – and then toss them a few morsels in between the regular feeds and observe them again. You'll see that they are much, much more inclined to snap up those odd morsels. Most experienced carp anglers are now persuaded that keeping the baits going into carp waters through winter, although in considerably smaller quantities, does much to keep the carp's feeding trigger primed and ready.

The low temperatures of a UK winter are tough for carp in that they have evolved in warmer parts of the world. If the winter is long and severe, conditions will be such that on most waters the carp feed very little, and must survive on their fat reserves. If these are insufficient then they will not survive. If they do survive, then they will still lose up to 15 per cent of their body-weight. We have been fortunate in Britain in that repeats of the extremely severe winter of 1963 have yet to recur. Many millions of fish died that winter from the total freeze-up, not just on still-waters but on rivers, too. Many thought that Redmire had lost virtually all of its big fish, though in the event that proved unfounded.

Other Feeding Triggers

Whilst it is vital to take into account the effects of water temperature on carp, whether it is going up or down, it is far from the only influence on whether the carp will feed. Temperature is one of the main drivers for dissolved oxygen levels in water; put simply, the higher the temperature, the less oxygen can dissolve. Low dissolved oxygen levels make the carp disinclined to feed. Nevertheless, two things can increase dissolved oxygen levels in water: the first is a ripple on the water, the second is the photosynthesis action of plants.

Late spring and a carp water recovers its green mantle.

The moonscape of this Christchurch Angling Club-controlled lake disappeared long ago, and today it is a popular carp water.

Gravel extraction stopped forty years ago on this Hampshire pit; the fishing has developed over the decades and it now holds carp to more than 40lb (18kg).

The effect of sunshine on water plants causes them to exchange carbon dioxide for oxygen, for the plant uses the carbon for growth. In darkness, the process reverses to a lesser degree and the plants breathe the oxygen. This effect may cause carp to seek oxygenating plants in sunshine, and to shy well away from them in the early hours of the night. Following a cold night it is often the side of a lake where the sun strikes first that attracts the carp, and in the evening the shaded side could be the one that receives most attention.

Wind has other effects apart from introducing oxygen, though this effect should not be underestimated. Many a water has come to life when a breeze has sprung up in hot, still conditions, and previously listless carp have started feeding.

Stronger winds, especially from the warm south-to-west quarter, can push the warm water of a lake into circulation and towards the windward end, and there is little doubt that at times the carp will follow the wind, at least for a short time. After a day or two the effect wears off, and the carp may become more widely distributed. None the less, be prepared to shift base if the wind does change.

What Sort of Waters Suit Carp?

From the foregoing, it is clear that waters that are warm, not too deep, alkaline and calcium rich and, most important, mature, are likely to suit carp best. Deep waters, acidic waters and new waters are least suitable. This doesn't mean they won't hold carp, but their potential for holding plenty of big carp is limited by one or more of these factors. In time, new waters mature. Their chemistry changes, they become more silty, and the banks gain the waterside cover of alders and willows. Lily beds and weedbeds develop, and the water gains character. The food chain develops too, and a water's potential may well improve with the passing of time. That doesn't mean a poor water will become a fantastic one, but given a helping hand through tree and weed planting, fertilization and stock management, its potential can be improved.

For very deep waters – clay pits are sometimes the worst culprits – there isn't always much that can be done as far as carp are concerned, and the best way to develop the water as a fishery may be through different avenues such as a bream fish-

ery. Similarly, very small waters may also have limited potential. Whilst waters as small as an acre can be astonishingly productive, ones that are much smaller than this have little capacity to hold many big fish. And if they do, it is all too easy to get the feeling of shooting fish in a barrel, and the sense of achievement when you do catch one is significantly reduced.

Two types of water that suit carp well are lakes formed by damming valleys, especially when the valley is fed by a chalk stream, and flooded gravel pits in river valleys where the water is alkaline. Damming a stream was the means by which many estate lakes were created over the last two hundred years, though there is always a risk that in time the lake will silt up completely, or that the dam will weaken and burst. The underwater characteristics of the lake tend to follow a similar pattern to the contours of the stream valley. A broadly triangular shape is common, the deepest water being usually found near the dam.

Gravel pits may come in all shapes and sizes. Their depth varies from the shallow ones that barely exceed 3 or 4 feet, to ones with substantial deep areas. As their water content is dependent on the water table you may find that the level changes through the years, with high water levels in winter and low levels in late summer. Gravel extraction is far from an exact science, and the underwater contours of the lake may be far from regular. The underwater ridges are known as bars, and are just one of the types of feature that may attract carp. Underwater ridges and hollows are often left together with islands, and these features offer the carp angler clues to the carp's whereabouts; the opposite scenario – a plain, featureless water whose cross-section is a simple saucer shape – offers little.

ABOVE LEFT: Clattercote is typical of many reservoirs that were formed by damming a stream valley.

This purpose-built French carp water has a carefully sculpted underwater profile, and therefore lacks the irregular underwater features of gravel pits.

3 CARP WATERS AND PRODUCTIVE SWIMS

The Different Types of Carp Water

Many thousands of waters in the UK hold carp, and these vary from tiny farm ponds to huge reservoirs and pits, from stillwaters to canals and rivers. The vast majority of carp fishing in the UK takes place on stillwaters, and they will be our main focus, as river carping is a more specialized topic. There still remains a huge choice of venues.

How much choice you have locally will depend very much upon where you live, but wherever that may be, these days you will have at least a few carp waters within reasonable distance. In some parts of the country the budding carp angler may not be so lucky as those in others, for instance the South, but this simply means that each individual should set his targets at what is realistic for his area, and should not set his expectations too high. Catching a twenty-pounder from a water in the far North can be just as satisfying as catching a forty-pounder from the deep South. All you need do is keep your expectations in perspective, and remember that the enjoyment is in the actual fishing for carp, which is the same wherever you fish.

No matter where you live, it will take time and research to discover what carp fishing is available. For some syndicate waters you will have to weigh up whether it is worth the greatly increased cost of joining, and then having to wait quite a long time, possibly a few years, to get a ticket. Even some clubs have waiting lists, especially those with sought-after waters, and an equally long wait could apply. The time spent on reconnaissance is seldom wasted; in fact, any time spent in planning, location and preparation is rarely a waste of time. Consider whether the water you'd like to fish offers the sort of fishing that you'd like to do: for instance, can you fish at night? Is it crowded with anglers casting all over the lake, making it difficult to fish sensibly without getting into arguments? How productive is the lake, and does it offer the chance of plenty of runs from high singles and low doubles – plenty of action to hone your skills? Or does it appear that the water is only heavily fished for the chance of catching one of very few monsters

Not every water holds carp as big as this one held by Mark, though big carp prospects continue to improve just about everywhere.

This 3-acre (1.2ha) French carp water has a deliberate big carp stocking policy. It contains few carp under 20lb (9kg).

that are rarely caught? Are the tales of big fish true? Or are they typical anglers' stories that grow with the retelling? Is it the sort of water where you can relax, watch the world go by, and catch some carp in peace? Inevitably there are lots of questions, and only *you* can find out the truth in the answers.

First, though, and it's worth repeating, decide on the type of carp fishing you *want*: is it lots of fish, but little chance of anything really big, but a great water to learn about the mechanics of carp fishing – casting, baiting and playing fish? Or do you want a middle-of-the-road water where you'll get enough runs to keep you happy and the outside chance of a much bigger fish, and where you can also learn a little about watercraft? Then there's the hard water, where runs are at a premium, but when you do get one there

is a good chance of it being a big fish, where the mechanics of fishing don't get too much of a run out, but watercraft, wiliness and the patience to wait are needed in abundance. It's your choice, but consider that even with carp fishing it is advisable to learn how to walk before you try to run.

An emerging type of carp water is the one that is tailor-made: this is likely to be 3 or 4 acres (1.2 to 1.6ha) and created from scratch. No other species is stocked, and initially the carp will probably be at least 10lb (4.5kg), with plenty of twenty-pounders (9kg) and probably some over 30lb (13.6kg). Because there is a high cost to setting up such a lake, this type of water is usually available on an expensive day ticket. Such a venue offers a short cut to catching big carp and can be compared to the average day ticket commercial fishery, but with big fish instead of the more usual smaller ones.

There is a drawback (though some would say it was an advantage) to this type of big fish commercial fishery, in that the stocked fish may well have never been caught before and are therefore relatively easy to catch. However, when the lake matures, with rich plant growth and, more important, when the natural food multiplies in plenty and anglers' baits become less necessary to the fish, they become much harder to catch and the fisheries become more like natural waters. However, this can, of course, be offset with prudent fishery management, with the continual stocking of new and not yet educated fish and the removal of any smaller offspring.

From all of this it is clear that the perfect carp water does not exist, or at least does not continue to exist over a prolonged period. Perhaps the best option is to get access to several waters, preferably ones that offer a variety of carp fishing, ranging from the difficult ones with bigger fish, to the easier ones that give you the confidence boost you need when you've had a prolonged period of blanks. Add to that a water that is just oozing with atmosphere, perhaps an old estate lake with lilies and other scenic plants, with not-too-difficult-to-catch carp residing in it, and you have a wonderful selection of carp waters to choose from.

How Deep are your Pockets?

With such a potential variety of waters available to the aspiring carp angler, it is clear that what he chooses depends on more than just what waters can be found in the area. You are unlikely to find 'free' carp waters, though there is always a faint possibility. Day-ticket waters vary from the 'cheap and cheerful' fiver a day, with the prospects of moderate sport for small carp, to ones that charge by the rod for all or part of the day. Some of these can quickly rack up a surprisingly high bill if you want to put in a longer session over a weekend. Others offer fun carp fishing that, provided you accept it for what it is, can be a good, low-cost way to hone your skills by catching plenty of carp on a variety of methods.

Angling clubs usually offer better value. Again, there is a wide variation in club fees, along with the waters and the type of fishing they offer. The membership fees could be as low as £20 a year, or as high as several hundred pounds; it all depends on where you live and the number of carp fisheries in the area. The more fisheries in the area the more likely you will find variety and lower prices – it's a case of supply and demand, as always, dictating the price.

Then there are the highly sought-after syndicate waters. These are usually quite exclusive, with low membership numbers relative to the acreage and the number of fishable pegs. The

It's not just day ticket and syndicate waters that produce big carp: this is Graham with a big carp from a club water.

emphasis with most syndicate waters is fewer but bigger fish, quiet and comfortable fishing, and with none of the hassle that can be experienced on many day ticket and club fisheries. Of course there is usually a hefty price to pay, of at least several hundred pounds per annum, and usually for just the one water.

Beyond this is the carp angler's dream (every angler's dream!): the chance to own, or to get the sole rights to, a secluded water from a friendly farmer or landowner.

None of these options, no matter how much you spend, will guarantee fantastic carp fishing, but the more research you do on your local waters, the more likely it is that you'll find access to the right waters for *you*, at a price you can afford.

Other Factors

Knowing what is available and at what price is only a starting point, for there are other factors to consider. You need the answers to questions such as the following:

- What is the head of carp like?
- How big do the carp grow?
- How far is it from home?
- What facilities are available?
- Is night fishing allowed?
- If so, how long can I stay for one session?
- How many rods can I fish at any one time?
- Are any of the baits or methods banned that I like to use?
- Can I use a bivvy?
- Is there safe car parking?
- Is the water crowded?
- Is there a problem getting into decent swims because they are always taken?
- Do matches cause disruption or even no access to the water at weekends?

Too many negative responses to these sorts of questions should make you reconsider your choice of water – though it may be that you have to accept some of them simply to get any local carp fishing at all. But maybe night fishing doesn't appeal to you anyway, and perhaps it doesn't bother you that the best swims are always taken because you are prepared to travel light to the farthest areas of the lake where you can find some fish as well as peace.

Finding Fish and the Best Swims

The ease with which you locate carp in a water varies enormously with the type of water, the conditions, the time of year, and the amount of time you spend actually looking. Most of the best carp anglers spend a lot of their time looking for signs of carp when fishing. And when they are not fishing, they still visit their waters and spend lots of time looking for carp. It can't be said often enough that finding fish is the most important aspect of any kind of fishing, for there is no doubt that the best angler in the world cannot catch fish that aren't there. On small waters you might never be much more than a long cast from the fish, and they can often be easily seen in clear water or when they're feeding or swimming at the surface. On small waters you will also observe signs of carp – whether it is bubbles, swirls, bow-waves or flat spots – provided you keep a low profile and keep quiet.

There are bubbles and there are bubbles … Visible fish activity is common in summer. Learning to recognize feeding carp from other fish activity is vital, and this is doubly so for bubbling fish. Many species of fish send up gas bubbles when feeding on the bottom, and it's a classic sign that there are feeding fish present. The most obvious ones are tench, bream and carp, though eels, roach, dace, crucians and chub can all bubble. Tench generally send up lots of pinhead bubbles in patches; this depends on the type of bottom, but is a starting point. Bream and carp both send up bubbles that are pea-sized. The big difference is that bream will often send up bubbles in a short line of a foot to two feet long. If you see an area of lake with a series of these lines in close proximity, then there is a fair chance that a shoal of bream is present.

What you need to find are patches of pea-sized bubbles, because these are most likely to be caused by carp. In shallow waters, very active carp can colour up the water, sending up clouds of silt as they grub around the bottom. Carp are certainly more vigorous feeders than both tench and bream. By close observation in waters where they can be seen you can learn to differentiate between the different fish present, so you will know what fish are in a water even when you cannot see them.

ABOVE: If you want to spot big carp close up, use cover like this tree, tread softly, and wear drab clothing.

Patches of pea-sized bubbles usually signify carp; lines of bubbles are usually bream; and pinhead-sized bubbles are usually tench.

Beware of being deceived by lake bed gas, particularly in estate lakes and those with a thick layer of silt on the bottom. Very often you'll see both small and large patches of bubbles that are no more than trapped gas escaping from the silt. Sometimes these bubbles can be almost indistinct in appearance from some fish bubbles, but the giveaway is that bottom silt bubbles are usually large and don't veer off as do the bubbles from feeding fish. Really, only experience of seeing bottom gas bubbles and feeding fish bubbles will teach you to tell the difference most of the time. But don't spend too much time fishing for bubblers unless you *do* know the difference.

Knowing the Water

Unless you are lucky enough to stumble across a water that has never been fished, or is so little fished that there is no available knowledge about it, there is a good chance that through observation of other anglers, and talking to other anglers and bailiffs, you can find out something about it. Such knowledge is not necessarily going to be given freely to all comers, but through a patient approach, determining as you go what is useful and truthful, you will find that most carp anglers will share some of the secrets of what they may rightly regard as 'their water'.

This is where patience and evaluation come in. Just because the first angler you talk to appears to know the water inside out and readily divulges its secrets doesn't mean that you now have a complete view of the water. As you will find out when you get to talk to other anglers on a water, there are many different views. Some anglers hide their own ignorance by appearing to know it all, others mysteriously tap their noses alluding to hidden secrets where there are none,

and worst of all are the fantasists who make up half their claimed catches, never weighing them properly and possibly giving a water a reputation for carp far bigger than actually exist. And sad as it is, there is a tiny minority of anglers who will tell you outright lies to try and ensure that you don't catch anything, and that you move to another water, leaving them to reap their ill-gotten gains.

As you gain acceptance from other anglers on the water, a little enquiring humility doesn't go amiss, and then you can start to sieve the truth from the myths and untruths. As you fish a pattern should start to emerge; favourite swims, effective methods and killing baits. Beware the absolutes: 'Floaters don't work 'ere, mate' or, 'Waste of time using anything other than boilies'. Such may hold true some of the time, but many anglers fall into lazy ways with fixed ideas. Once that happens the idea of experimentation is lost, and catches result from sheer rod hours regardless of the effectiveness of swim choice, tactics and method.

Very old lakes such as this estate lake often have extensive lily beds.

On waters larger than a few acres there may be areas that are hardly ever fished; they may be too far from the car park, too uncomfortable or too snaggy. Yet this may be the very area that you need to get a better understanding of. Just like anglers, carp can be creatures of habit, too. Whilst certain areas of a lake and some swims may be hot, there is always a danger that the constant fishing pressure makes the carp living in those swims very wary albeit well fed. Elsewhere on the lake a pioneering approach could reap dividends but only if you understand where, when and how. Sometimes the hotspots develop through convenience and reputation rather than actual results. Their nearness to the car park and consistency in at least producing some carp give the false impression that they are better than they really are. Put some time aside and make the effort to fish the less popular spots and it could pay dividends.

Pay attention to the most successful anglers on a lake, subtly of course, for there are some who won't thank you for quizzing them or blatantly spying on them. But they can't stop you from watching them from a distant swim. Try to find out what makes them successful and why their results are so consistent. They may not, initially anyhow, seem to be doing anything a great deal differently than the consistently less successful anglers, but they may be particularly adept at, for instance, choosing the right swim in certain conditions. If that is the case then note which area they fish when the wind is in a certain direction, or which bank they are more inclined to fish when there is no wind. However good the method and bait they use, they have to be presenting it consistently in the right swims. Don't fall into the trap of thinking all the best anglers have a secret bait. Most carp anglers do indeed have at least one bait that they wish to keep to themselves, but it won't be the bait alone that is responsible for their success, it will be the right combination of location, method *and* bait.

The Features of a Water

What are features? They can be anything that gives the water character, changing the fishery from being a plain, saucer shape in cross-section, with nothing growing on or around the margins. Features can be islands, underwater shelves, holes and gravel bars. A feature can be the vegetation both in and around the water, such as reedbeds, rushes, lily beds, sunken or overhanging trees, tree roots and weedbeds. It can describe natural feeding areas such as bloodworm beds where silt has accumulated, or simply a bay off the main lake. Any or all of these can be potential carp holding areas. Although some features may look the fishiest places in the world, they rarely hold carp, or at least rarely hold feeding carp. That, incidentally, is another thing to be aware of, that some carp holding

This shallow area around an island has a variety of carp-attracting features including weedbeds and shallow, warm water.

areas are not necessarily carp feeding areas. There are plenty of waters where the carp have a resting or holding up spot, but where they never seem to feed.

It is a fact that carp spend a great deal of time near features and margins, and are more likely to feed in such places. Open, featureless water may have carp passing through, and there are instances where the carp are driven far from the bank by disturbance there, but getting them to feed confidently out in the open can be more difficult. There are exceptions to this, with one good example being where there is a breeze picking up on the open water in hot conditions and the carp seek this more oxygenated water, and may be catchable on long-range floaters. Generally, however, there are far more carp within 4 or 5 yards of the bank, and not necessarily the bank furthest away from you if you have polished your skills of being quiet and stealthy.

Sometimes you will come across a water that seems to be one huge feature: there are immense weedbeds, rushes, sunken trees and gravel bars just about everywhere, but it can be a case of too many features spoiling the choice for both the carp and the angler. As always, location is the key.

Hot Swims and Hotspots

On any heavily fished water, certain swims become established as 'hot' swims, yet just because you have claimed such a swim, maybe for the first time, it is important to know that it may have one or more very tightly defined hotspots. Where there are apparently numerous 'hot' areas that could hold carp, you still need to find the hotspot within that area, for it is a fact that almost all likely swims have a small area within them that will get you more fish than anywhere else. The problem with most of these hotspots is that, other than lying somewhere within a general feature, they don't usually have anything different to identify them. They're just a relatively small area that is well worth finding, and the only way to do this is to use your second or third rod to fish different areas of the feature until it becomes clear that one particular area produces most of the runs. When you find it you can fish at least two of your rods there, and exploit it as much as possible.

It may well be the case that unless you can feed extremely accurately and present your bait in the correct spot, your chances are much reduced. This applies to big fish of many species. It doesn't mean that unless your bait is in the hotspot you will never catch fish, just that it is less likely. In angling, 'always' and 'never' are dangerous words; don't expect the fish to read the rules! Remember that hot swims may only fish well in certain conditions or at specific times of the year. The reason it is currently vacant could be that it is simply not fishing well at present, a fact known to the regulars.

Open, Featureless Water

A word of caution; don't dismiss open, featureless water. Although some kind of feature usually defines a good swim, there are often areas of open, featureless water in most carp fisheries that consistently produce lots of fish. They have nothing about them to set them apart from any other swim, and most likely the area will have been discovered by accident. Occasionally you will discover one of these areas for yourself, usually due to arriving at the water and finding all the feature swims occupied, forcing you to fish an unpopular, featureless area and then finding that one of your rods, in a certain spot, enjoys more than its fair share of runs. Make a careful note of its location for future reference, for this could be one of those areas where, for no obviously apparent reason, carp consistently feed.

On the other hand you may discover one of these featureless hotspots by design. They're usually discovered as you fish elsewhere and observe fish rolling or crashing through the surface in a distant area. You notice that the fish show regularly in one particular spot, and you make it your business to fish that spot either then or on your next visit. You can't pinpoint the exact spot when you fish it, as your feature-finding exercise reveals that there is no feature. So you fish and observe again, and when the fish begin to show you cast to the disturbance, clip up the line, make a note of a far bank feature to cast towards and you've cracked it; another hotspot is discovered.

Bars and Shelves, Plateaux and Holes

It is true that many man-made waters are even-bottomed, with little in the way of underwater features. This is especially true of modern commercial fisheries. Larger waters that have come about from the flooding of disused clay and gravel workings are often much more irregular. Those operating the machinery to extract the gravel and clay are principally concerned with extracting the minerals in the most efficient manner rather than leaving a perfectly sculpted lake. It is little wonder that all manner of steps, inclines, ridges, holes, hollows and bars are left behind. When the pit fills with water and becomes a lake an interesting underwater landscape forms. In time, these underwater features change as underwater erosion and siltation soften the contours. But they still remain as features.

Where the bottom slopes downwards then levels out, it is known as a shelf. Such a feature is significant for many bottom-feeding fish, and carp are no exception. Carp often follow regular patrol routes near the bottom of the shelf where

Despite the rope preventing anglers casting into the very snaggy area beyond it, this swim is a carp hotspot.

BELOW: *These carp are easily spotted as they swim in shoal formation over dense weed.*

food has collected. Carp, like most fish, use their swim bladder to stabilize their buoyancy, and small variations of 2 or 3 feet make little difference to this buoyancy; but imagine a lake where there is deep water of 15 to 20 feet that is interspersed with much shallower bars that almost come up to the surface. These shallow areas might only be 2 or 3 feet deep. The carp cannot rapidly change their swim bladder buoyancy from the ideal for 15 feet to that for 2 feet or vice versa. The carp will not keep changing depth on their regular patrol routes, but will be more likely to stick to more or less the same depth. So there are times when they will be in the uppermost layer of water, just under the surface, and willing to feed in shallow areas on waters where there are these big variations in depth.

For the most part, then, it can be the more subtle variations in depth that provide the hotspots, making it all the more essential to learn how to map a water with some accuracy.

Weedbeds

Carp may frequent many types of weedbed. Weedbeds offer them cover, food and extra oxygen. Classic weedbeds are water lilies that may take one of several forms. The rarest is the dwarf lily with tiny 3in (7cm) pads, but much more common are the ornamental lilies with flowers in various colours and floating pads. These afford the carp shade and cover, as well as food in the form of clumps of snails' eggs attached to the underside of the lilies. Less common on lakes is the wild yellow water lily with its cabbage-like underwater leaves (known as 'cabbages' to anglers) as well as floating pads.

Carp like being in and around lily pads, and this gives you the chance to sneak up on them to drop a free-lined floating bait on the edge of, or even amongst the pads. This type of fishing is heart-stopping sport and usually demands somewhat heavier tackle. When the carp discover the floating baits you must keep still, but the moment you get a take you will need your wits about you, as the fish is likely to plunge immediately, deep into the lily bed.

A number of other types of weed are found in abundance in lakes. Broad-leaved pondweed (*Potamogeton*) is another common weed that carp favour. Canadian pondweed is a strange weed in that it can often take over lakes; ironically, carp can reduce its impact by actively eating and uprooting it. But where there is Canadian pondweed in abundance, its presence will create problems for bait presentation. Also, where the bottom of a lake is muddy or silty and the carp stock in the lake is generous, the feeding activity of these carp is enough to prevent abundant weed growth. The feeding activity has a knock-on effect, in that the mud prevents sunlight from penetrating the water, and plants rely on sunlight (photosynthesis) to grow. A well established water with little weed growth and permanently cloudy water is a sure sign that the water has a generous stock of carp that feed regularly.

There are plenty of carp around these weedbeds.

Reedbeds

The most common marginal plants are reeds and rushes of different kinds. These reeds are able to take root in shallow water so their presence signifies shallow water with an increase in depth close by. Norfolk reed is similar to a miniature bamboo cane. Carp frequent reedbeds of this type, and can be detected through the reeds shaking and moving as the carp move between them. Norfolk reeds are tough and capable of cutting even fairly strong line. Three other types of reed occur; these are the bulrush, which consists of elongated tapered British racing green stems and is found on gravel; the great reed mace, which has the characteristic brown club seed head and grows on mud; and sweet reed grass, which is like a giant grass and only grows in the shallowest of water.

Although tiny reedbeds have little merit for carp fishing, wherever there are extensive reedbeds, especially Norfolk reeds or great reed mace, and a reasonable depth of water – 2 to 4 feet – then you will likely find carp. Apart from the cover and protection, there is much natural food on the reed stems, and therefore all the more reason for the carp to stay around.

Although the water is shallow alongside reedbeds, they often attract carp.

Trees and Bushes

It is common for scrub willow and alder to colonize disused gravel pits and other stillwaters, and for fishery owners to plant trees as well. Willow is prone to growing into the water, and with some owners felling trees as well, bankside cover is plentiful. You can be sure that at least some of these swims will hold carp, which instinctively feel safe there. You will often find that most of the actual growth is above water, but be prepared to find plenty of sunken branches and roots that constitute major snags should a carp plunge into them.

Islands

Islands may be accidental leftovers from the digging of a pit, or created deliberately to add an additional margin to a lake. Because it is rare to be able to gain access to an island, they represent an undisturbed marginal area. Add in overhanging trees and bushes, and rushes, and you have a perfect carp hotspot. Sadly, it can be such an obvious carp-fishing target that there is often a tendency to fish such areas to oblivion with the carp so wised up to the dangers of feeding around the margins of the island that other areas are actually more productive, especially when targeting the biggest carp in a lake.

Channels

Not all islands are regular oval 'blobs'; some are irregular and fragmented. There may be channels between the islands or even between adjoining lakes. Often, too, clumps of reedbeds, both large and small, will grow out from the actual margins, leaving channels between them. Carp are very much an exploring fish, and will know these channels and short cuts intimately. Whilst the actual cut-through may not be a defined feeding area, it can be worthwhile to bait a channel on the basis that the carp have to pass over or close to your baited patch when swimming through it. Some narrow channels can be excellent ambushing spots when they form part of a carp's regular route.

Margins

Marginal areas are the most overlooked yet productive areas of most carp lakes. They are simple to fish – no long casts, easy to feed quietly and accurately, and yet challenging for all the wrong reasons.

The main disadvantage to fishing the margins is too much disturbance from other anglers. The fish will come within a couple of feet of the bank given half a chance, yet persuading them to do so can be beyond the patience of many, or beyond

These fallen trees provide a safe haven for big carp: getting them out could prove difficult.

ABOVE: Small islands provide an undisturbed margin area that is exploited by carp.

This channel through the reeds is used by carp to get from one part of the lake to another, and offers the possibility of ambushing them through careful feeding and accurate casting.

As a result of stealthy feeding there are 30lb (13.6kg) carp feeding just inches from the bank here.

their ability to stay quiet and keep a low profile. One type of water where margin fishing really can score is busy day ticket fisheries that *don't* allow night fishing and all anglers must be off by dusk. It is often the case that most anglers arrive reasonably early, and begin to pack up in late afternoon. As they do so, they chuck the remainder of their bait into the margins. The carp, especially the bigger ones, soon cotton on and move right into the margins in early evening when the majority of anglers have left. Whilst the bigger carp are willing to feed avidly, it doesn't follow that they are necessarily easy to catch, but simple float fishing with the bait a couple of feet from the bank and the angler sat well back can be surprisingly deadly. When you do land a fish you need to have a low disturbance routine that involves keeping very low with the lightest of foot movements, and ideally returning the fish a safe distance from the swim.

Bloodworm Beds

Many waters accumulate layers of silt that may provide ideal conditions to support vast colonies of bloodworm. Bloodworms, the blood-red inch-long larvae of mosquitoes, are a favourite food for most bottom-feeding fish, and carp are no exception. Carp are adept at rooting in the mud for food, and may become preoccupied in feeding on bloodworms, muddying the water as they do so. It is often the case that although there may be a

number of silty areas in a lake only some of them are ideal for bloodworm. Aside from conventional carp baits, it is worth considering using a bait that resembles super-sized bloodworms – a small bunch of redworms for instance. Very often, when you find a big patch of bubbles indicating intense feeding activity, it is usually carp feasting hungrily over a bed of bloodworm.

Unfortunately they can also be the most difficult fish to catch in spite of you knowing exactly where they are and that they are feeding avidly. The problem, as already mentioned, is that they can become totally preoccupied with this highly sought-after natural food and absolutely refuse to take anything else when harvesting the bloodworm bed. Perhaps not so much refuse, but blindly ignore any other type of food in the vicinity. Even bunches of bloodworm in mesh bags won't do it, for the carp are switched on to feeding on the bloodworm by rooting for it in the bottom (hence the bubbles) and are totally 'blind' to anything else. But don't let that stop you trying to catch them, for just occasionally a carp will 'slip up' and find a hook in its mouth.

Mapping a Water

Mapping the water could lead to you finding a pattern that you can take advantage of on future sessions. At its simplest you can make a basic sketch of the outline of the water, noting trees

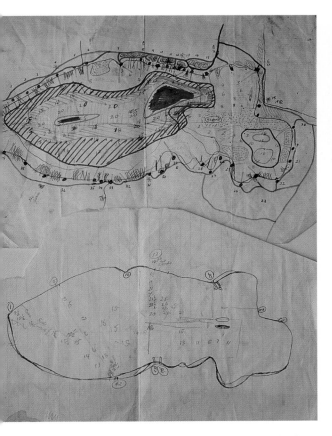

Mark created these maps thirty years ago using depth-finding floats (top map) and from a boat with a 50ft (15m) tape measure and lead (bottom map).

Ian Gemson shows a typical marker float set-up.

Feature Finding with a Marker Float

and weedbeds. At its most detailed it can be done to scale based on Ordinance Survey maps, and further refined using the likes of Google Earth. Then, by plotting in depths, features, hot swims and places where you have seen carp or know where they have been caught, you can build a complete picture of the water.

The most accurate depth, bottom contour and bottom make-up plotting is done by using a rowing boat or a baitboat with sonar fitted, and to some extent using the old-fashioned method of using a plumb line from a boat. Alternatively, on smaller waters or where boats are not allowed, it is possible to get a good idea of depths, contours and the bottom make-up by using rod and line and a marker float. Use of a marker float is the most common method of depth and feature finding.

To find depths and features with a marker float you need to use a rod and reel that will cast the float and lead at least as far as you can cast with your carp rods. To make things easier you can mark the butt section of the rod with lines 6in (15cm) apart, or purchase one of the purpose-made marker rods that are now readily available. The beauty of a specifically designed marker rod is that the tip is softer and will therefore be more sensitive to the feel of the lead as it trundles along the bottom.

The reel should be filled with buoyant braided line of around 20 to 30lb bs, the diameter of which is less than 8lb mono. Braid is best due to its non-stretch property, for unlike mono it will better transmit the feel of every pebble on the bottom.

Make sure the marker float you use will cast straight, is very buoyant, and is easily seen. The

Korda ones are ideal and you can choose different shapes, sizes and colours to suit different conditions. Most leads will work satisfactorily for feature finding, but if you want maximum 'feel' then the pear-shaped watch leads, generally known as gripper leads, or those specifically manufactured for feature finding, such as the 'Grubber' lead from Wychwood, are the ones to use.

Choose as heavy a lead as you can get away with, as the weight will help you to read the feel of it better, and will help prevent it skipping over smaller objects on the lake bed.

Set up the marker float with a short length of thicker braid, say 12in (30cm) of 50lb bs, coming from the lead, and then tie in a swivel or a run ring. Thread the main line through the link eye or run bead, then through a large rubber bead, and then tie it on to a link clip. Now clip the marker float to the link clip, making sure the main line slides freely through the swivel or run ring. By using the link clip you can easily change marker floats for a different colour should the light change, or for a bigger or smaller or different shaped float if necessary.

Feature finding with a marker float involves much the same procedure, initially, as when lining up the rod to make consistently accurate casts. Choose a reference point along the far bank, or something on the distant horizon – anything that doesn't move, like a particular tree or an electricity pylon, for instance. Don't use a cow or a sheep as there is a good chance it won't stay in the same place (joke! Although it has happened ...).

Make a couple of casts to get the feel of it, and then cast to the reference point, and as soon as the lead hits the surface, close the bale arm of the reel and take up all the slack so that you can feel the lead as it sinks. 'Feel' the lead down with the tip of the rod held fairly high, and wait for touchdown. Pay attention to this as it is your first indication of the bottom make-up. A firm knock indicates rocks or gravel, a muffled thump is clay or firm sand, a softer touchdown could be weed or silt.

To measure the depth, make sure the float is pulled right up to the lead, holding the line close to the first measurement line on the butt section, pull line through your fingers until you reach the 12in (30cm) measurement line, and continue to do this until the float appears at the surface, counting each time you release 12in of line, plus

any spare inches at the end, using the 6in (15cm) measuring line. You can make a note of this depth in a notebook, and compare it to depth checks emanating from that first reference point. In this way you will have a clear picture of any shelves and bars, and just how much they vary.

Once you have a clear idea of where you want to fish, you can then cast to the far side of the area and slowly draw the lead along the bottom, standing side on so that the rod tip is being pulled at right angles. Feel the vibrations through the rod tip and try to interpret the differences, remembering that firm, 'clattering' judders on the tip usually mean gravel, and the softer ones mean silt or soft weed; 'snatchy' soft pulls with occasional jumps usually mean thicker weed. Don't draw the lead along by winding the reel, but by drawing it slowly with the rod tip, and then reel in any slack before you make the next draw.

Much of the latter on marker float work and feature finding demands experience before you can read all those touch-sensitive signals. You're not going to be able to make overly accurate readings until you've had plenty of practice, so don't expect too much too soon. Persevere though, and if possible, make a visit with someone with experience who can feel the different signals and then hand the rod to you so that you can feel it too and know exactly what it is you're feeling. Depth and feature finding are one of the most useful things you can do to consistently catch carp, so it pays to make a point of learning how to do it.

A gripper lead will help you 'feel' the make-up of the lake bed.

4 BAITS

Baits in Context

Baits for carp can be as simple or as complex as you want to make them. Many anglers stick to one or two tried and tested baits, never venturing beyond them, and still consistently catch carp. Alternatively, you can study the subject and gain a deep understanding such that you are able to devise new and possibly unique baits that could give you an edge over anyone else – that is always the dream, anyhow! Baits for carp are a vast subject, but by breaking it down into manageable chunks, it will become less daunting.

Think of baits in terms of those that can be both hookbaits and feed baits, those that are best as hookbaits only, and those best suited to feeding; within these groups there are four main subgroups. First we have traditional and natural baits such as bread, worms and maggots; particle baits such as sweetcorn, hemp and maple peas; boilies and pastes; and finally fish feed pellets and their derivatives. Just to add to the variety there is also the increasing use of artificial baits that are made of plastic and other synthetic materials: extraordinary as it seems, they do catch carp.

From this already extensive list it is clear that carp will, at some time, eat just about anything edible provided they are able to recognize it as food. Some natural baits such as water snails, bloodworms and earthworms are instinctively recognized as food. If you tried to catch the carp in an unfished pool using conventional baits such as bread, you might well find that it took a while for them to become accustomed to recognizing the bread as food. They would not be suspicious of it, merely unaware of its food potential; but curiosity as much as anything, and a wild creature's natural instinct to test anything for food potential, would soon teach them that bread was good to eat.

Even in heavily fished waters carp are quick to take advantage of a few slices of bread scattered on the water.

Once the carp accepted the bread and you began to catch them consistently on it, the next problem you would likely encounter is that some of the carp would become suspicious of it, realizing that eating it sometimes resulted in a trip to a landing net. If you were using floating crust, for instance, the carp might carefully mouth the crust to test for foreign objects and odd behaviour, rather than gulp it down as they did in the early days of using bread as bait. They might knock the bait around, trying to break it up or dislodge it, testing to see whether it behaved differently from the other free-floating pieces. This is a very early stage of carp becoming educated, but it is easy to see that despite the multitude of baits, no matter how sophisticated, there is always going to be the challenge of persuading the carp to accept our baits without arousing their suspicion.

It's much the same with boilies: there is no doubting their effectiveness, indeed they have become one of the most successful carp baits of all time, but in a natural food-rich and unfished lake, it could take some time for the carp to really switch on to them. Much natural food consists of organisms that are much smaller than a typical boilie – bloodworm and tiny snails are typical – and the carp just don't recognize the much larger boilies as edible. A period of prebaiting boilies and other non-natural baits is always an advantage, but where a little fished or unfished lake is concerned, it can be essential.

To our advantage as anglers, carp are greedy fish that will feed vigorously in warm conditions, and even in cold conditions will be willing to feed spasmodically. Furthermore, certain foods contain appetite-triggering chemicals that carp recognize, albeit unconsciously, and these will stimulate them into feeding. Carp are also visually attracted to feed items, and this is where bright baits such as sweetcorn and the rather bizarre fluorescent pop-up boilies can score.

Preoccupied Feeding

Many fish feed in a way that can be described as preoccupied; it is simply a natural response for a wild fish to take advantage of an abundance of food that is usually due to seasonal events. For example, the annual mayfly hatch on chalk streams causes trout to become preoccupied with eating them; and carp become preoccupied with eating bloodworm, daphnia and other tiny food creatures at those times of year when they're abundant.

Consequently, if anglers introduce small particles of bait in generous quantities it is hardly surprising that fish can be weaned on to the taste of them and then become completely focused on eating them, almost to the exclusion of anything else. The advantage to the angler of such a baiting method is that the fish need to feed hard to get

These pom-poms are an unlikely yet potentially effective carp bait when flavoured.

The convenience of modern carp baits cannot be overstated.

sufficient food to reward the effort. Also, the pre-occupation with this bountiful food larder is so strong that at times it suppresses their natural caution and they suck up the baited hook as readily as the free offerings. Part of this 'throwing caution to the winds' can also be due to competing with other fish, for the treasure trove may have attracted fish from far and wide. This is one of the reasons that what seem to be 'old-fashioned' baits such as maggots, casters, hemp and other small particle baits seem to work forever, whereas a bait such as a bright pink boilie might work briefly, then fail.

There Are No 'Magic' Baits

Anglers have been searching for the ultimate, irresistible bait since the first worm was impaled on a bone hook. Forget it, there are no magic baits. There are only effective ones, with some more consistently effective than others, this effectiveness depending on several factors. If a bait has been heavily used on a water to the extent that many carp have been caught on it in the recent past, then there will come a point where its effectiveness is likely to wane. However, that does not mean that it will never catch carp from that water again. Maybe someone will introduce a new bait that the carp will get accustomed to, and that bait in turn will become the new 'wonder' bait on that water. In time, the carp will forget about being wary of the old bait, and perhaps two or three years later the old bait will regain its effectiveness, for a while at least.

Other Factors in Bait Choice

Not only must a bait be acceptable to the carp, it also needs to be suitable for presentation on tackle strong enough to land carp. Whilst a match angler might present a minute bait such as hemp seed or bloodworm on a tiny hook with ultra-fine line, such a set-up is unsuitable for carp, which need much larger hooks and stronger lines. This doesn't totally preclude small hookbaits such as maggots and casters, but we do have to think carefully about how to present them. Many carp baits are ideally matched to carp tackle: boilies, for instance, which can be any size from about 10mm to 30mm (⅜in to 1in), are the right size to match to carp gear – though mounting them directly on the hook is not a good idea as hooking power is compromised, a problem easily solved by the hair rig.

ABOVE RIGHT: With boilies as bait you don't have to use a single one all of the time; sometimes multiples of two or more are better.

Tempt carp, even big carp, into feeding confidently enough, and they'll come in very close – provided you don't scare them.

One of the problems of bait choice in any type of angling, not just carp fishing, is that many baits are non-selective. Maggots are one of the least selective baits of all, appealing to just about every freshwater fish that swims. Yet in the right place they can be a deadly carp bait. And even boilies, designed to defeat bait-robbing tiddlers, often prove attractive to bream and tench of about 1lb (0.45kg) upwards. So how do we get around this seemingly intangible problem?

On waters where there is a great variety of species present you may have little choice other than to use boilies, often in the larger sizes of 20mm and bigger, and learn to live with the fact that sometimes you will catch other species. But waters that contain nothing but good sized carp do exist, and this gives you much more scope to experiment with baits.

The effectiveness of different baits varies considerably with the seasons and water temperature. By making the appropriate choice at the right time you can improve your results, rather than by trying to make one bait work regardless of conditions. The other extreme of never giving any bait a chance to work properly is not a good option either. You need to test each bait's effectiveness through giving it a thorough trial, but only when you have a good idea that it is going to work. Sometimes to do this may mean going against the accepted wisdom on that water, but bear in mind that many anglers, perhaps even the majority, are lazy in their habits. Once they've had some success with a method or bait they tend to stick with it, even though a change to something else could improve their results.

Although boilies have become synonymous with carp fishing to the point where the majority of carp anglers use nothing else, it is vital to realize that situations do arise when an alternative bait offers a better chance of success. There are times when other baits can outfish boilies to an extraordinary degree. Where boilies do score is in their ability to remain effective for many hours, to defeat the attentions of bait-robbing tiddlers, and in their convenience. But for the short-session angler, prepared to use methods other than standard bolt rigs, and unworried by having to re-bait frequently, these advantages lose effect. And therein lies one of the disadvantages of boilies in that they tend to be slow baits, which is all right for slow fishing but not when you've only got a couple of hours to fit in. This is when you need a bait that will get results quickly – depending on the fishery of course, for there are some difficult lakes with a small head of very big fish, where the only realistic mode of attack is via the luxury of time and a bait that will remain on the hook for long periods.

Flavours

All baits have some sort of flavour, varying from barely detectable to outright pungent. Many consistently successful carp anglers have spent decades trying to determine which flavours are the most effective. Despite this extensive research, the findings are inconclusive. There are times when a bait with very little flavour works well. 'Washed-out' baits, those that have been in the water for as long as twenty-four hours, can be the most effective of all, but this could be due more to the carp being wised up to the apparent 'safety' of such baits, rather than it

OPPOSITE: Top-quality bait and a simple rig helped Graham land this 35lb (15.8kg) carp.

Try boosting the attractiveness of your bait with a glug.

being much to do with the lack of flavour. There are other times when the complete opposite works – glugging or soaking already highly flavoured hookbaits in a concentrated pot of flavour. Mostly, there is a consensus that flavours should be added at the recommended dosage when concocting a bait mix; in other words, try not to overdo the flavouring. Flavours used to excess often repel carp rather than attract them, and many experienced carp anglers prefer the flavour of their baits to be understated rather than overstated.

Then there is the question of what flavour is best. There are sweet flavours, savoury flavours, fruit, meat and fish flavours, and some that defy description. Some baits other than boilies and pellets have little natural flavour, though this can be changed with the addition of a bait flavour, with maggots and casters falling into this category. It is likely that naturally occurring amino acids trigger feeding responses in the carp despite their subtlety.

The way in which these flavours work varies, too. Some are oily in nature – the oil that floats off hempseed is an example of this. Others are water-based, and may leach out quickly. It is generally accepted that oily baits are best for the warmer months of the year, though there is little substantiated evidence to support this. A number of experienced carp anglers have studied bait flavours in considerable depth and can blind you with the science of appetite stimulators and feeding triggers. That is not in the remit of this book, however, and besides, too much pseudo-science regarding baits will serve more to confuse the issue than to clarify it. Many anglers, including the authors of this book, are great believers in keeping it simple, and our advice is to use proven fish-catching flavours in subtle amounts. And if in doubt, leave it out.

Traditional Baits

The traditional baits as far as coarse fishing is concerned are bread, maggots and worms, though for carp there is a somewhat long history of using flavoured bread pastes (with natural ingredients such as honey) and partially boiled potatoes. These baits (other than bread paste and potatoes) remained favourites for a long time for good reason: they catch fish, including carp, and can sometimes outfish the most sophisticated of baits. Where they can score is that they are likely to be accepted quickly by the fish and are the nearest thing to an instant bait. This makes them ideal for short, opportunistic sessions where the fishing is relatively easy and at close range. For the angler who doesn't have the time or inclination to catch really big or difficult carp, then, given the right water and conditions, using these traditional baits with simple traditional gear and methods can be just as much fun as an ultra-modern, high-tech approach using boilies.

These baits are ideal for what can be termed as 'fast carping'. When you are snatching a few hours fishing in a summer evening after work you often don't have time for a method that could take six or eight hours or more to work. Baits such as maggots and casters can enable you to catch carp very quickly, especially if you time your sessions to suit likely feeding times and conditions.

That is not to say that traditional baits don't have their disadvantages. First, they are mostly unsuited to fishing much beyond close range; they are also non-selective in that they will catch almost all other freshwater species, too; and they are less durable than boilies in that you must replace them on the hook rather frequently. It is no good baiting a hook with bread flake in the evening and expecting it still to be on the hook four hours later: fifteen minutes is far more realistic, which is exactly why re-casting every ten or fifteen minutes is much more realistic when short-session float fishing using bread.

Maggots

Whilst maggots are associated with catching small fish, and by implication small carp, there is no doubting their effectiveness in catching carp of all sizes. Their small size means that carp can become preoccupied with them, yet once the problem of presenting them on a suitable rig has been overcome there is no reason why you shouldn't confidently fish for carp with maggots.

Maggots are best used on waters where nuisance fish are largely absent; one excellent example is where a new water has been created that contains only carp. The carp in such waters often respond better to a mass particle bait such as maggots, initially at least, rather than boilies, which need more time to become the dominant bait.

For fishing for carp of modest size – up to 10lb or 12lb (4.5kg or 9kg), say, in snag-free water – it is possible to use what is best described as barbel gear, and present maggots nicked on a size 14, 12 or 10 hook. To use bigger hooks than this for much bigger carp we need to find a way to attach a bunch of maggots to the hook without nicking them on directly, as the thicker wire of the hook will burst the maggots. One way is to superglue the maggots to a plain, loopless hair on a hair-rigged hook. Use the tiniest dab of glue on the stumpy end of the maggot and stick it to the hair. Subsequent maggots can be glued on in the same way, or glued to an adjacent maggot. A word of caution though: be extremely careful you don't glue your fingers to each other, to the maggots, or to the hair!

Another more popular method of fishing maggots on big hooks these days is to use the Korda Maggot Klip that comes in three sizes. These are tied to the hair, or hung on the hair loop, and the maggots threaded around the Klip. Because maggots tend to crawl away and disappear into the mud when fed into a swim, it can be a good idea to use dead ones. The easiest way to do this is to suffocate them in a plastic bag, freeze them for at least twenty-four hours, or scald them with boiling water. Use maggots killed this way within a day or two as they turn black fairly quickly.

Casters

Casters are an underrated carp bait. Carp find them even more attractive than maggots, but the downside of casters is two-fold. They are more expensive than maggots, being typically 30–40 per cent more expensive, and are even harder to keep in good condition. They are also more fragile, and therefore difficult to mount on hooks bigger than about a size ten. They can be superglued to a hair, as with maggots, and mounted on a Korda Maggot Klip, but it's a delicate operation and for most anglers, hardly worth the effort. For the casual carp angler fishing a small club water for a short evening session for moderately sized carp, casters can be a deadly attractant bait that are easy to present on simple float tackle.

Worms

Worms can be an instant carp bait. Perhaps their most useful application is as a free-line bait, or

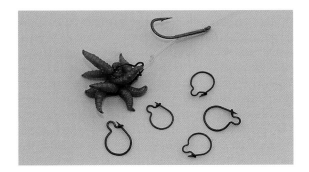

ABOVE RIGHT: Using a Korda Maggot Klip offers a convenient way to present a bunch of maggots on a hair rig.

Old-fashioned and often ignored, worms remain a good carp bait particularly well suited to stalking techniques.

presented under simple float tackle to carp that are feeding greedily in muddy shallows. The carp are expecting to find food such as bloodworms, and a small bunch of redworms or a lobworm is close enough often to fool the wariest of carp. They are certainly not a bait to disregard. Chopping up worms into small pieces has long been a means of triggering a feeding response from carp.

Bread

Carp need little encouragement to feed on bread, though its disadvantages make it best suited to fun carp fishing or surface fishing where, on some waters, it can still be deadly. For simple leger or float tactics bread flake – a chunk of bread pinched from a fresh white loaf and lightly pinched on the hook shank – is ideal. For surface fishing, a chunk of bread crust hooked on a large hook is worth a try.

The disadvantage of bread is that it isn't especially robust, so is unable to withstand casting, other than a simple lob, and is fragile against the attentions of other smaller fish. After a short while, ten or twenty minutes, it becomes soggy enough to all but dissolve, and the novice's greatest fear when using bread, that the hook is baitless, is soon realized. Using floating crust has similar disadvantages: once the crust is soggy the carp can easily knock it off the hook for a free meal. This isn't always a bad thing as it may increase the carp's confidence to take the next bait offered.

Seeds

Seeds include sweetcorn, hemp, peanuts, tiger nuts, tares, maple and peas. Whilst there is no doubting the effectiveness of hard particle baits such as various beans, peanuts and tiger nuts, problems linked to fish deaths, whether actual or perceived, have led to many fisheries banning them. However, if prepared correctly they can be a deadly bait on most waters and pose no problem to fish welfare. It is incorrect preparation, the seeds and beans not being soaked and boiled for long enough, that has led to them continuing to swell so that they block the carp's digestive system.

The method of preparation is to half fill a large container with the bait, and then cover with cold water. Leave to soak for fifteen to twenty-four hours. Top up with cold water if necessary, place on a stove and bring to the boil; then simmer for thirty minutes. Drain off the water and allow to cool. Session-sized portions can then be bagged up and frozen.

All beans and nuts can be hair-rigged and fished like boilies. Popped-up nuts can be fished by using a buoyant artificial nut along with one or two real ones, or by mounting a piece of foam on the hair between two real baits. Incidentally, most particles work best when you feed the swim with a generous amount of the particle in use.

There are several seedbaits that you can use to great effect, mainly as feedbait but also on the

Simply hooking through the bait and pulling it back in is still the best way to fish floating crust.

 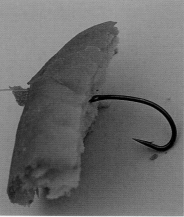 

hook. These are hempseed, tares, maple peas and sweetcorn. These last two are easiest to use on the hook, but tares and hemp can be superglued to the hair. At one time you were restricted to buying the dry seeds from pet shops and seed merchants, but the superb quality of ready-prepared seeds from companies such as Dynamite Baits makes this unnecessary.

Pellets

It didn't take carp anglers long to spot the carp bait potential of the pellet food used to fatten up rainbow trout in fish farms. More than forty years ago, thinking anglers found that crushing the hard, fishmeal-based pellets into powder made the basis for an attractive paste or an excellent boilie mix. For many years, the pellets were only available in small sizes, generally 3 or 4mm. Tiny 1mm super-rich pellets for feeding salmon and trout fry are also available, and can be an incredible feed for drawing and holding carp in a swim.

What triggered a pellet revolution was the manufacture of much bigger pellets for the farming of halibut. These high in oil pellets are made in all sizes from 2mm up to 'donkey chokers' of 25mm (1in). It soon became clear to carp anglers that not only was a new attractive feed-bait available, but here was one big enough to be drilled and mounted on a hair rig as a hookbait.

The robust nature of these pellets meant that they would last for several hours in the water, like a boilie. Since then their use has spread to rivers where many anglers use them for big chub and barbel, as well as accounting for numerous big carp, tench and bream in stillwaters.

ABOVE RIGHT: Sweetcorn is ideal for adding to spod mixes and is still an effective carp bait, though it is not especially selective – bream and tench can be a nuisance.

Pellets remain a firm favourite as a feed bait for carp fishing; many are specially formulated for carp fishing.

The dark coloration of halibut pellets (remember they are for feeding halibut, not made of halibut!) is indicative of their high oil content. Despite their effectiveness, it is becoming clear that used to excess – a difficult thing to define – the dependence of fish stocks on such an oil-rich diet leads to the fish packing on layers of fat. Coarse fish may also struggle to metabolize them and excessive use could lead to fish deaths.

Asking anglers to use highly effective baits in moderation is a little like telling the tide not to come in – a futile gesture. Simply banning them is likely to prove unpopular. Fortunately, bait manufacturers have come to the rescue. Recognizing that certain elements of the fishmeal pellets are highly attractive to carp and other fish, yet also realizing that the extreme oil content can be significantly reduced, they have created a wide variety of far more carp-friendly pellets specifically for angling.

Pastes and Boilies

The idea of using some form of paste as a fishing bait goes back centuries. The simplest form is either a paste made with stale bread, or by mixing flour with water. The result is a soft attractive bait that can be enhanced with the flavour of your choice. Historic angling books mention adding honey to make the paste more attractive. The great advantage of a paste bait is that it can be easily formed to cover the hook without masking the point; you can use a tiny pellet smaller than a pea, or a great dollop the size of a walnut.

When carp fishing started to develop along more modern lines in the post-World War II years, bread paste was one of the key baits together with parboiled potatoes and lobworms. These baits were good at the time but nothing like as effective as the next generation of high protein pastes and the subsequent development of the modern, commercially available, boilies and pellets.

Initially, anglers made carp pastes from cat and dog meats, tinned sardines and tuna, and other varieties of tinned meats and fish that inventive carp anglers sought out in the supermarket. These were flavoured with curry powder and other exotic flavours, also off supermarket shelves and found on the stalls in ethnic markets.

This period in carp bait history was followed by the modern era when carp bait became an entity in its own right. The idea of developing much more sophisticated pastes with better flavours that would be more attractive to carp developed in the late sixties and early seventies. Alongside this, the idea of developing pastes that provided nutrition to carp also evolved. It was reasoned that carp would, by preference, choose baits that were more nutritious over less nutritious ones. In seeking suitable protein bases for their baits, pioneering anglers such as Fred Wilton and Gerry Savage were discovering the ingredients of the common carp baits of today.

As various powders were incorporated into pastes to increase their attractiveness, some disadvantages emerged. These were principally that pastes tend to completely dissolve relatively quickly, often in a matter of minutes, and secondly that their soft nature makes them vulnerable to small fish nibbling the bait. In other words, within a short time you could not be sure that you still had bait on your hook. Seeking to improve the durability of these pastes, some anglers experimented by mixed their pastes with egg white. This proved a better binder, but it was

Pastes like this one are a useful float-fishing bait for big carp.

OPPOSITE: Mark used a shelf-life boilie to tempt this 26lb (11.8kg) carp.

adopting the method of immersing balls of paste in boiling water for anything from 30 seconds to 3 minutes that provided the desperately needed breakthrough. The boiling water 'sets' the egg in the mix so that the boiled bait has a tough skin – tough enough to hold the bait together and defeat the tiddlers, yet the bait is still attractive to, and eaten by carp. The boilie was born. And once the hair rig was developed, the problem of mounting a round tough ball of bait on the hook was solved.

Pastes

There is still a case for using pastes for carp fishing. They are ideal for the carp angler who wants to quietly float fish in the margins, accepting the need to rebait frequently. Also, pastes are better known as a boilie wrap these days, and are used to do exactly what the name implies: to wrap around a boilie. The advantage of fishing paste, or a boilie wrap, in this way is that you have all the initial attraction of a paste oozing flavour, and the robustness of a boilie beneath that skin for the carp to suck into its mouth.

The choice of pastes is wider than ever. You can concoct your own based on ground-up trout pellets, mixes of processed meats and bread-crumbs, or boilie mixes without the boiling part of the process. Alternatively, you can buy pro-prietary paste mixes or ready-made pastes in tubs, and use these. Most carp anglers simply retain a portion of the boilie mix to use as a boilie wrap.

Boilies

Boilies have become the bait of choice for most modern carp fishers, and it's easy to see why. Their effectiveness, coupled with convenience, and the fact that they work extremely well and keep on working, have made them the bait of first choice on most waters. Furthermore, the modern carp angler is spoilt for choice of top quality baits that catch big carp consistently, amongst the best being Sonu Baits, Quest Baits, Spa Baits, Nutrabaits, Richworth and Mainline.

Boilies are excellent for both hookbait and feed, used either whole, in halves, or crumbled and fed via PVA string, bag or a spod. The round shape is also very good for firing from a catapult or throwing stick.

They are available in, and can be made in, var-ious sizes, the most popular size range being 14 to 18mm. Smaller sizes, such as 10 and 12mm, are usually used to tempt smaller carp, or in multiples to tempt wary larger carp that have seen too many boilies of 'standard' size. Use larger boilies of 20 and 25mm for very big carp, or to deter bait-robbing fish of other species.

Boilies can be made to either sink or float. Sinking boilies are the most popular, as these can be used for both hookbait and feed. Floating boilies, better known as 'pop-ups', are used as surface baits or, most often, as baits that hover some few inches from the bottom – popped up. They can be used on their own or in combina-tion with a sinker as a critically balanced bait. Sometimes a combination of a sinking boilie with a smaller pop-up boilie on top, known as a 'snowman', can be deadly.

Boilies are usually made with one of three basic ingredients: a 'cheap' base mix consisting of a 50/50 mix of semolina and soya flour, a fish-meal base mix, or a bird-seed base mix. It is said

This pop-up rig uses heavy metal tungsten putty to pin it down at the hinging point where the braid is stripped back.

Broken and crumbed boilies are often used as feed.

that bird-seed mixes are best for winter and fish meals best for summer, although in reality both will catch at all times of year. Various additives are used, including amino acids, minerals, appetite triggers/stimulants, oils, flavours and colours. Certain well-established flavours such as Tutti Frutti, Scopex, maple, strawberry, squid, liver and the old favourite monster crab have stood the test of time and remain favourites with many successful carp anglers. But if you intend to make your own bait, have fun experimenting; that's part of the appeal of making your own bait, especially when you catch on it!

There are two ways to obtain boilies; buy packs of frozen or shelf-life ready-made boilies, or create your own by mixing your chosen ingredients, including eggs or water, to which you've added a flavour, rolling the resulting paste into balls, and then boiling for the required time.

For many anglers the convenience of using readymade boilies outweighs the advantages of creating your own, and many carpers have realized that the extra effort of mixing, forming and boiling the baits doesn't necessarily create a superior bait to those available off the shelf. Although it must be said that there are also many carpers who do believe that a fresh boilie is superior to a shelf-life one, so the jury is out on this one too. However, the main advantage of creating your own bait is that you may come up with a boilie that is unique to you and is therefore less likely to 'blow' (a carping term to signify the bait has been identified as dangerous by the carp),

and so it is possible it will catch more fish for a longer period – although it is becoming less likely that a unique bait is produced these days when so many are taking that route with more or less the same basic ingredients. If you are interested in getting heavily involved in developing your own baits it is worth seeking out a specialist book on carp baits, for it is a vast subject – *see* the Bibliography for further details.

Air-Dried Boilies

If you go the convenient route the choice is between frozen and shelf-life boilies. Each has its advocates. Frozen baits tend to be softer, whereas shelf-life baits are tougher; indeed, if left long enough they can become like bullets. In fact, one process to change a fresh or frozen boilie into a shelf-life one without the use of preservatives is to air dry them. Once air dried they are an excellent deterrent for beating bait-robbing tiddlers, crayfish and the Poisson Chat of French lakes, and they can be left in water for twenty-four hours or more without breaking down.

You can buy a mesh bag especially for this job, but any type of bag with a weave small enough to contain the boilies and allow air to flow freely over them will do the job. Another way is to lay them out on mesh trays. The longer you leave them, the harder the boilie will become, and the longer it will last both in and out of the water. A convenient way to 'air dry' frozen boilies is to bury them in a bag of trout pellets for up to three weeks. The pellets absorb the moisture in the boilies. The disadvantage of this method is that the boilies take on some of the flavour of the pellet, which may not be what you want.

Shelf-Life Doubts

Some carp anglers question the wisdom of using shelf-life boilies, wondering if the preservatives used make the boilies less appetizing than preservative-free freezer-life boilies. There may be some truth in this, but not to the point where there need be any fear about using shelf-lifes, for there have been thousands, if not millions, of carp caught on them over the years.

Another more recent question has been the effect of the preservatives in shelf-life boilies on the health of fish: do the preservatives do them any harm? Some recent research suggests that this is possible, though common sense and history suggest otherwise, especially considering that the same preservatives are used in our own food. It's yet another question about baits we won't know the answer to until more thorough research is done.

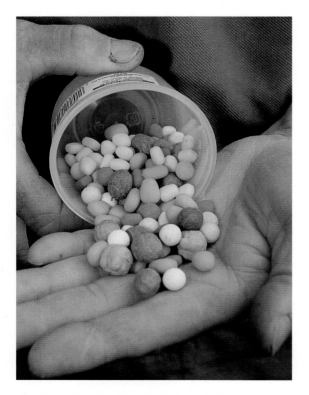

A wide variety of artificial baits is available.

> **Bait Colours**
>
> Ask the question of ten experienced carp anglers which bait colour is best, and you could get ten different answers. Some swear by bright colours, saying they attract carp, while others swear by dull, drab ones, saying that bright colours repel carp. Yet others will say specifically that red or orange or yellow is the best colour. None of them is right and none of them wrong, because all colours of bait catch carp. Maybe some colours catch better on dull days and others on bright days. The best thing to do is to experiment on your own waters at different times and see what you come up with. Just remember that most questions to do with bait are subjective; there is no ready answer.

Artificial Baits

Believe it, they work! Plastic imitations of sweet-corn, tiger nuts, boilies, maggots and so on, very often work used on their own, but most often when used in combination with the real thing. Most artificial baits are buoyant, which means they can be used as surface baits or pop-ups, or used to critically balance combination baits. Use your imagination!

Groundbaits and Spod Mixes

Groundbait

Groundbait for big carp is not a popular method, though goodness knows why not, because it can be quite deadly. Probably it isn't so popular because it is so much easier just to take along a bag or two of pellets and boilies and fish over a bed of those: no mixing to do, and no mess.

Groundbaiting for carp of mid-double figures and upwards needs to be different to the groundbait normally associated with small, commercial fishery-size carp. Groundbait for these bigger fish should, at least to some extent, feed them rather than merely attract them, which means the groundbait needs to have some body or bulk to it, and include ingredients that the carp can actually feed on. The basis of the mix can be crushed brown and white crumb, which you can purchase anywhere, and it needs to be bulked up with pellets, crushed pellets, sweetcorn, hemp, maize, broken boilies and boilie crumb; it can be further bulked up with the carp angler's favourite dog food, Vitalin, particularly if you expect to be using a lot of groundbait. The water you mix it with can be flavoured with, for instance, some thick, syrupy CSL (Corn Steep Liquor) or an oily additive. The groundbait should be a much stiffer mixture than that for smaller carp and other species.

What you want to achieve is for the carp to attack the balls of groundbait hard enough to break them down into pieces small enough to fit in their mouths. Big hungry carp will do this with no problem at all, though they'll have to work at it, and this in turn will make them hungrier. You can't fill big carp as easily as you can fill other species and smaller fish, so there is not much danger that you can overfeed them. Besides, when fishing for bigger carp the idea is to catch one or two big, wily fish rather than a bag of smaller ones, and there is every chance you will do just that as the carp pick up the nearby hookbait as they attack the balls of feed.

The above mix is suitable for both heavy groundbaiting by hand or catapult, and as a Method mix, although it is better to make the mix a little on the softer side if feeding by hand within throwing distance.

ABOVE: Put the dry ingredients of a groundbait mix together, and mix thoroughly before adding water.

A good spod mix: fishmeal-based groundbait, sweetcorn with mashed tuna.

Spod Mixes

A spod, sometimes known as a bait rocket, can be used to deliver accurately any kind of bait to any distance you can cast to, whether long or short range. Spodding has become the carp anglers' first choice baiting tool. Although there are proprietary spod mixes you can buy off the shelf, such as Sonu Baits Spod Mix, made of various flavour-enhanced pellets, you can actually spod any kind of bait from loose groundbait to loose feed, or just a handful of boilies. Combinations of particles such as hemp, lupins, tiger nuts, peanuts, tares, chick peas, maggots, casters, chopped worm and so on, all make good spodding fodder.

Many carp anglers will spod out a liquid mix to put a cloud in the water, popularly known as spod soup; this mix is a combination of small particles such as hemp, minced tuna, salmon oil and, for instance, condensed milk and other flavours. It should be mixed so that it is sloppy and drips off the fingers, but is not too runny. Perhaps a thin porridge describes it best.

The most popular spod mix is a combination of pellets, crumbled and broken boilies and whole boilies, to which you can also add hemp, corn and maggots, particularly dead ones. Many carp anglers like to spod a wide variety of baits so the carp find a food table that is so diverse they don't become preoccupied on any one thing and pick at everything. Use a spod in combination with a marker float to provide a target to form a food table in a precise spot; a spot that is like a magnet to the carp, and so appetising they will linger over it for long periods, picking away at the diversity of food on offer.

One thing to remember is that small particles will spill out of the spod when it's in flight if you overfill it. Approximately three-quarter full is about right. Also, mix a little groundbait to plug the spod after filling; not too tight or it won't release the feed easily enough after casting.

A stunning Common is returned from the weigh sling.

5 TACKLE: RODS, REELS AND LINES

Today, carp gear is an entity in itself, tackle that has been specifically designed to catch carp, unlike other coarse-fishing tackle that covers a greater spectrum and is usually not species specific – although in the case of barbel, often referred to as the 'new carp', barbel gear is going the same route. The sheer quantity and range of carp gear must be mesmerizing to a beginner, and can't be much better for the experienced angler who is thinking of specializing in carp fishing.

Apart from a huge range of rods, varying in length and strength, and of course price, and a large variety of reels, there is an absolutely massive range of accessories to make the carp angler's fishing easier and more comfortable. The modern carp angler is kitted out not only for fishing, but also for longer stays at the waterside. Today's carp angler is usually a 'session angler', who generally fishes overnight and very often for several nights. It is not surprising, then, that much of the carp angler's kit is there to provide protection from the elements, warmth, comfort and refreshment. Modern carp angling, especially for the bigger, harder-to-catch fish, is as much to do with sessions that are longer than normal as it is to do with fishing.

What you also need to understand is that you will be buying two, if not three, rods, reels and lines. Carp anglers who fish with only one rod (unless stalking fish, or floater fishing) are rare, and no matter how much you may convince yourself that one rod and reel will probably suffice in your quest to catch big carp, it will not be long before you realize that a pair of rods is the minimum requirement. It's not just a case of doubling your chances by having two rods, it's being able to fish more than one spot, and being able to try more than one bait and method at any

one time. So if you're new to carp fishing it's as well to be prepared for the extra outlay and to realize that fishing two rods at the same time is a minimum necessity, and that three is most likely. Given bottomless pockets it is easy to equip yourself with the best carp gear that money can buy, and such is the quality available that there is a good chance of getting a top class outfit. However, such an approach may cost you thousands of pounds yet still not be entirely satisfactory.

The major items you will buy are rods and reels, and although lines are a much more minor item in value, they are very important in practice. So it makes sense to devote this first chapter on gear to rods, reels and lines, including shock leaders, and the next chapter to all the other accessories you'll need for a complete carp-fishing outfit. Terminal tackle and rigs deserve a chapter to themselves. It is important that you understand enough about carp gear design and function to enable you to make informed choices, and can budget according to your finances yet get excellent value for money.

It is true that with some of the larger manufacturers you could just about completely equip yourself within one brand, and be completely happy with what you had. Nevertheless, a pick-and-mix selection across several manufacturers will probably do the job even better and save you money as well. In this way, you can take advantage of each manufacturer's strengths and end up with kit that not only works well, but also feels good to use. Gear that feels right will make you a more confident angler. When you hit a run you need to be certain that your tackle will not let you down, that your reel is reliable and that your rod is as good at playing fish as it is at casting.

Rods

The simple way to buy carp rods is to buy two or three matching rods that will probably do the job according to the manufacturer's advertising. Three 12ft (3.6m), 2¾lb test-curve rods will tackle most carp-fishing situations with few problems. As long as they are not too cheap and are from a reputable maker, then they ought to be capable of casting up to a hundred yards or so and playing big carp in most situations. And that is exactly what most carp anglers require.

But it doesn't explain why some carp fishing is better tackled with a lighter rod, or a shorter rod, or a more powerful one. Carp rods are designed to be jacks of all trades, with a range typically starting at 2½lb test curve and going up in ¼lb increments to 3¼lb test curves, with perhaps a 4lb test curve specifically for spodding. Sometimes you will find a carp rod with a lighter test curve such as 2¼lb, or heavier at 3½lb, but the most popular ones have test curves of 2¾ or 3lb. Some carp fishing is better tackled with a lighter rod with a test curve of less than 2lb, but more of that later.

In sixty years carp rods have progressed from being very flexible built cane, 10ft long and with a test curve (TC) of 1½lb, through slightly less flexible fibreglass at 11ft and 2lb TCs, to the

For long-range fishing this powerful 3¼lb test-curve rod will punch out a baited rig well over 100 yards in the right hands; it is less user friendly for playing fish.

This budget-priced 2½lb test-curve rod has far less casting potential, but is much better for playing fish.

modern, much stiffer carbon-fibre rods, typically 12ft (3.6m) long with 2¾lb to 3lb TCs. That is quite a progression. Rods are longer, stronger, less flexible and more powerful, matching the need to tackle bigger carp at much longer range.

It is clear that you need to get a good understanding of the type of carp fishing that you intend to do, so that the rods you buy are well matched to the waters, the distance you want to cast, and the size of fish you expect to catch. It is all too easy to read an article where the author recommends carp rods with a test curve of 3¼lb, and you then find that with experience these are destroying the pleasure you get from playing the

fish. A rod needs to act as a casting tool, a vital characteristic, but it must also act as a playing tool that is comfortable and pleasant to use. A rod that is too powerful for the size of fish being caught will not have enough 'give' to absorb the lunges of the played fish.

On the other hand, being significantly under-gunned by using a rod that is much too soft for big fish has the opposite effect, in that there is simply no power left in the rod to have any effect on the played fish. This means that the fight will be too prolonged, overtiring both the fish and the angler. Worse, you will have nothing in reserve to prevent a hooked fish reaching snags.

What is a Test Curve?

We have already made mention of test curves, yet what exactly is a test curve? How is it measured, and is it that important?

The test curve of a rod is a means of giving a rough guide to its power. It never has been an exact science, and is less so with modern high modulus carbon blanks, and despite two different rods having exactly the same test curve, their characteristics might be very different. How a rod bends is important: a rod that bends mainly in the tip section is said to be fast-tapered, whereas one that bends throughout its length is said to be through-action.

To measure the test curve of a rod, the butt is fixed horizontally with the reel in place. The line is threaded through the rings, and weight added to the end of the line to load up the rod until the tip is at an angle of 90 degrees to the butt. This loading is the test curve, and it gives a useful guide to ideal casting weight and line strength, though top class modern rods are immensely versatile. The ideal casting weight is fractionally more than 1oz per 1lb of test curve, so the ideal casting weight for a 3lb TC rod would be about 3 to 3½oz. Ideal line strength (monofilament) is similarly easy to calculate, being approximately five times the test curve.

These simple figures indicate that understanding the sort of carp fishing that you are generally doing is worthwhile so that you are neither under- nor overgunned. There is little point using a 3lb TC rod on a small water where the carp average 6lb (2.7kg) and the biggest is barely 10lb (4.5kg), and the maximum cast required is no more than 30 yards. In these circumstances a lighter rod, perhaps an Avon or barbel rod with a TC from 1¼ to 1¾lb, would be more suitable. Conversely, tackling a big pit, where the fish are much bigger and long casting is required using PVA bags and heavy leads, is going to require something much beefier – a rod with a test curve of at least 2¾lb, possibly more.

Mark piles on the pressure using a standard barbel rod. On this water, most of the carp are in the 7–10lb (3–4.5kg) range, making this rod ideally suited.

When a rod is ideally matched you will get the best of both worlds: casting is straightforward and accurate, and playing fish is something you can feel confident in enjoying, knowing that your tackle is adequate for the job yet responsive enough for you to enjoy the experience.

A Rod's Test Curve

The test curve (TC) of a rod is still our best guide to the power of the rod, but the old reckoning is now almost invalid. Here's a quote from Dick Walker, who knew a thing or two about rod building, regarding the TC of a rod when built cane was the material of the day:

> It should take up the curve that brings the tangent to the tip at right angles to the tangent to the butt when the load is about one-fifth of the breaking strain of the line that will usually be used, the pull required to do this being known as the test-curve loading. A latitude of about thirty per cent either way in line strength, and more in skilful hands, can be allowed.

Walker designed his built-cane Mk IV carp rod at 1½lb TC to take lines from 6lb to 12lb. Today, a carbon-fibre rod built from the best grade of materials, which is classed as having a 1½lb TC, will have a much greater latitude than that, particularly at the heavier end of the scale. Some rod manufacturers have now begun to rate rods by casting weight, but this measurement is just as loose as the test-curve measurement. This inexact science is testament to the strength, flexibility and tolerance of the modern rod-making material: high modulus carbon. For instance, when the strength of a Daiwa Longbow carp rod was demonstrated on Daiwa's 'Terminator' machine on a visit to their factory, lifting a dead weight of 16.5lb (7.5kg), it was clear that the latitude of modern carbon rods is a great deal more than any of us realize.

In reality what it means is that a carp angler with a preference for making the most of playing a fish, and who requires a rod that is flexible throughout its length, can still cast, say, a 3–4oz (85–113g) weight with a 2¾lb TC rod – perhaps not quite as far as a 3lb TC rod would, but certainly far enough. And it would do so without any fear of the rod breaking. So bear in mind,

modern rods are extremely tolerant, and you can use rods either side of the optimum parameter to satisfy a particular preference for flexibility, or the lack of it.

Dr Stephen Harrison of Harrison Advanced Rods, like Daiwa, one of the few rod blank designers and manufacturers in the UK, also says that the test-curve system is flawed:

> In practice the problem of pulling tips to ninety degrees with a ninety-degree pull probably seemed academic with a cane Avon or Mk IV carp rod. The test-curve method worked in a practical sense for flexible, forgiving cane rods. But as rods have got more powerful and materials have changed from cane through glass to carbon, the problems of measurement have increased dramatically. The high modulus tip of the modern rod is more reluctant to follow the line to ninety degrees.

We do wonder if there is some other guide we can use that will give us a more accurate idea of the playing *and* casting power of a rod, and also a good idea of its action. Dr Harrison wonders the same thing, and says:

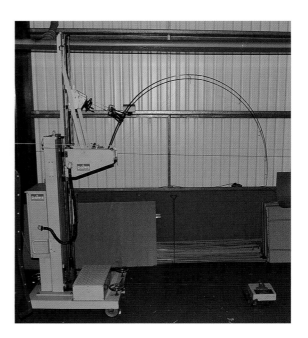

Daiwa's 'Terminator' test rig is a significant factor in their ability to manufacture incredibly tough carp rods.

In the past I have discussed this problem with many people, but so far none has come up with a solution. What we need is a measure of how much line a rod gives during flexing as a result of a pull by a fish. Imagine a rod clamped in a fixed position so that we could measure deflection against force of pull. If we were to plot on a graph the amount of line given, or deflection of a rod, against pull or load, we would get a curve. This curve would vary from rod to rod according to the action. If we can find a simple way to describe this curve, then we would have a measure that indicated both power and action. The curve of deflection against load would have a faster rate of change, a steeper ramping up, than a through-action rod, which would be closer to a straight line.

Different manufacturers try to get round the problem in different ways. Some stick to the old test curve, others describe their rods as being 'suitable for lines of xlb bs', whilst yet others say a rod will cast a weight up to xlb. None of them tell us exactly what we want to know – that is, casting and pulling power and action. But for now, the test-curve rating is still the best, albeit rough, guide.

Price Reflects Quality

A quick glance through the tackle adverts in the press or on the Internet will reveal that carp rods can be obtained for as little as £10, though the cheap ones are usually around £30, and from there through all the price ranges up to in excess of £300. They can't all be the same quality, so what is the difference?

The principal component of a rod is the blank, which is usually made from a carbon-fibre composite. The quality of the carbon fibre varies enormously; in simple terms the finer the cloth, the more expensive it is. The better rods are made from cloth that is more expensive. The very cheapest rods are made from a cloth that is a mixture of carbon fibre and glass fibre, and the very cheapest might best be described as glass-fibre rods, containing only enough carbon for it to be legal for them to say it is a carbon composite. Even some mid-range rods that cost between £50 and £100 have significant glass-fibre content. The giveaway on this is the weight of the rod. A rod made from a high grade of carbon fibre is very light; this applies to all rods – match rods, carp rods, fly rods, barbel rods – because as the proportion of glass fibre increases, so does the wall thickness of the tube and so does the weight.

In addition to the quality of carbon fibre used, the taper of the rod and how well that taper has been designed also changes the quality of the rod. The compromise between casting (fast taper) and playing (slow taper) must be reached. Here the better quality of the carbon fibre plays another part. When you cast you impart a lot of energy into the rod, which is released during the cast. Top-class carbon does this very efficiently, and recovers from the bend very quickly; the poorer quality ones much less so. This means that a better rod can help you cast more accurately and with less effort.

Length

The majority of carp rods are 12ft (3.6m) long and made in two pieces. A few are 13ft (3.9m), useful for fishing at very long range but otherwise of little advantage, and a few are 11ft (3.3m) long, though mainly at the lower end of the test curves at, say, 2¼lb. For most carp fishing, 12ft-long rods are ideal and their only significant disadvantage is that being in two pieces that are slightly longer than 6ft (1.8m), you may find it difficult to get them into a small car. The exception to this general length for carp rods is special stalking rods that are often just 9ft (2.7m) long so that you can wield them in a confined space.

Rod Rings, Handles and Other Fittings

Most carp rods have five main rings plus an end (tip) ring, and this configuration is the ideal compromise between casting and playing ability. The fewer and larger the rings, the less friction on the line when casting, but taken too far would mean acute angles of line between one ring and the next when the rod is bent into a fish.

The inserts for the rings may be silicon carbide (SiC), aluminium oxide or titanium oxide. Whilst the SiC inserts are the most expensive they are the most prone to developing line-shredding hairline cracks. The greatest risk to carp rods ringed with SiC rings is from

For stalking, a short specialist rod with a test curve of 2¾lb is ideal for manoeuvring in tight spots.

accidently dropping them on hard gravel, easily done on many gravel pits.

As for the reel fittings, perhaps the best advice is that it is worth checking that the reels you intend to use fit the rod snugly and securely, but up- or down-locking, screw-fit reel fittings are now pretty much standard.

The high gloss finish on many carp rods will reflect the sun, and if you ever decide to do some stalking the reflections could be enough to scare the carp. A coat of durable matt varnish (Humbrol is good for this) will fix the problem, as will a rub with wire wool, being careful only to remove the gloss and not rub through the varnish to the bare blank.

The Standard Rod Set-up

There are many tactical approaches to catching carp, but the standard set-up is with two or three rods on a rod-pod fitted with bite alarms. This somewhat depends on the circumstances and rules for the water. Having decided upon your ideal carp rod for your intended fishing, it makes sense to have matching rods and reels. This means that whichever rod produces the run, you are utterly familiar with it from the moment of striking the run without having to pause and then adapt to that particular rod and reel.

Depending upon how versatile and involved your carp-fishing intentions are, you may see that other rods could be useful for carp fishing.

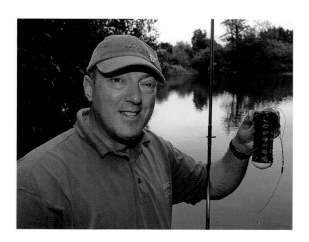

To cast a fully loaded big spod like this you will need at least a 4lb test-curve 'spod' rod.

Sticking to mainstream carping, the first consideration is a rod for 'spodding'. This involves launching a large plastic rocket-shaped capsule of bait to the baited area. As this capsule will weigh in the region of 10 to 12oz (280 to 340g) it is clear that normal carp rods do not have sufficient strength to achieve the range and accuracy required. Many ranges of carp rod follow the normal range of 2¼ to 3¼lb TC with a 4lb TC special spodding rod. If your budget won't run to even a cheap spodding rod, then there are alternative baiting strategies including mini spods, PVA bags, stringers, Method feeders and plain old-fashioned catapults.

For fun carp fishing, a decent 12ft (3.6m) barbel rod with a 1¾lb test curve can be used for close-in float fishing, lightweight Method work or lightweight floater fishing – and you can always use it for barbel fishing!

Reels

Reels for carp fishing have evolved into two standard forms: the free spool, large size fixed spool reel, and the very large size 'big pit' reel. Other types of reel can be pressed into service for carp fishing, including standard fixed spool reels and centrepin reels, but let's look at the main types in depth first.

A fixed spool reel, which is the standard carp fisher's reel, has several functions: it stores the line, allows long casting, and aids playing the

Standard carp reels such as this Shimano Baitrunner are excellent for most short-range carp fishing.

fish. Carp fishing refines these functions and adds a further one – the ability to feed line during a run without opening the bale arm. Lines for mainstream carp fishing are commonly from 10lb breaking strain and upwards, and therefore a reel for carp fishing needs to have the capacity to store these larger diameter lines. That means large-size spools, and increasing the proportions of the reel accordingly. Large spools and good line-lay aid long casting, and this is taken to the ultimate with the big pit reels, which are made on an even larger scale with the addition of longer spools.

The demands of reeling in large weights and playing big fish put considerable stress on a reel, so it is vital that it is robustly built to withstand this. The drag mechanism on modern reels is highly efficient and capable of being fine tuned. Some are on the front of the spool, known as front drag, and others are at the rear of the reel – rear drag. Which type is best is open to debate, but provided the one you choose is smooth and doesn't snatch, then it should be fine.

Previously the only way to allow a carp to run was to leave the bale arm open and use an elastic band or line clip to trap the line against the rod to prevent it peeling off the spool. Then some canny carp angler discovered that maintaining some tension on the line as the carp was running led to far fewer throwing the hook. Graham applied this tension by stuffing a tapered chunk of foam into the butt ring. Then free-spool reels were invented by Shimano: they called them 'Baitrunner', and the word 'Baitrunner' has become as synonymous with free-spool reels as 'Hoover' is to vacuum cleaners. Similar mechanisms on other makes of reels have brand names such as 'bite n' run', 'bite runner', 'free spin', and so on.

The free-spool reel uses a mechanism operated by a lever on the reel body that instantly disengages the drag on the spool without losing the pre-set tension that you have applied to the drag. This allows the spool to spin freely as the fish runs. The drag is re-engaged by turning the handle of the reel, or flicking the free-spool lever back to its 'off' position. An amount of drag can be applied to a running fish by adjusting the tension on the free-spool. Being able to adjust this tension is also useful when you want to maintain a tight line to the lead and to prevent undertow, or flow in a river, from giving unwanted turns.

Free-spool reels come in various sizes, and to make matters even more confusing there is no universal numbering system. Daiwa and Shimano, two of the largest manufacturers of reels, use similar systems for reel sizes. Generally, carp reels start at around the '5000' size and go up to the '10000' size. For short-range fishing with line in the lighter ranges, and where you are unlikely ever to cast more than 50 yards (46m) or use a weight heavier than about 2oz (57g), the smaller sizes are most suitable.

Big Pit Reels

For extensive long-range work and the biggest carp, by far the best option is to get big pit reels, not surprisingly named thus because they were originally used on big gravel pits. These are reels with big, long, tapered spools to facilitate very long casts. They are also usually a much more robust reel that will handle casting heavier weights and retrieving heavier loads. They were, and indeed still are in some cases, surf-casting reels. Today though, many are made specifically for the carp-fishing market. The early models did not have a free-spool mechanism, and the procedure was simply to loosen the drag on the front knob, lift into a running fish by clamping one hand over the spool, and then tighten the drag to its previously set position. However, the modern big pit reel has a type of free-spool mechanism built into the spool, whereby an inner wheel sets the drag and an outer lever instantly releases or re-engages the drag.

The best big pit reels are very expensive compared to standard carp reels: their much grander scale means that the engineering is upgraded to match, and hence the price rises steeply with it. Thus, whereas typically good quality free-spool reels are obtainable in the price range £50 to £120, the big pit reels tend to be in the £150 to £400 range (at the time of writing). Quality tends to come at a price. Many cheaper reels are adequate for the casual carp angler, but may work out more expensive in the long run because they simply do not last that long.

For longer-range fishing a big pit reel is needed.

The Shimano X5500 combines the large line-carrying capacity of a big pit reel with the dimensions of a standard carp reel.

They may also be more frustrating to use for various reasons: the drag may not be so smooth, or the reel may be prone to tangles, or because the line-lay is not so good, you may find it difficult to cast the maximum distances. Big pit reels are generally big and heavy, but one big pit reel, the Shimano Ultegra 5500 X-TB, known as the 'mini big pit' reel, is something of a compromise and is surprisingly small and light compared to most other big pit reels.

Other Reel Options

The other options for carp-fishing reels are mid-sized standard fixed-spool reels that are around the '4000' size. These are fine for short-range float fishing or floater fishing, especially when tackling small to medium-sized carp using lighter rods and lines than the norm. Couple a reel like this with an Avon or barbel rod, and you will have a well balanced set-up.

In similar vein for close-in margin fishing, many experienced anglers like to use a robust centre-pin reel. Avoid the more delicate models that are better suited to trotting: you want one that is strong enough to be loaded with 10 or 12lb line. Using a centre-pin for carp fishing takes some skill, but is easily learned with practice and, barring the occasional friction burn on your fingers if you're not careful, is great fun for playing carp.

Lines

There are several important aspects when choosing a line for carp fishing, and lines that rate as good main lines are not necessarily the best for hooklinks, so they will be dealt with separately.

Main line for carp fishing must have several important qualities. It must be obtainable in a suitable breaking strain, which generally means the range 8–18lb, although 12–15lb main line is the norm. It must be limp enough not to continually spring from the reel spool in uncontrollable coils, but must be robust enough to withstand abrasion from gravel, tough weed and other snags. It must be resistant to rapid deterioration through prolonged exposure to damp and sunlight. Unless required for surface fishing where a floating line is advantageous, it should sink easily. It must also knot well. Finally, it must be obtainable in lengths of at least 200 yards, or better still on bulk spools that hold sufficient to fill three spools in one go, at reasonable cost. Fortunately, line manufacturers have understood these qualities for many years, and it is not too difficult to find bulk spools of top class line at very reasonable prices.

There are further qualities that a main line could have, which break down into three types of line: standard monofilament, fluorocarbon and similar derivatives, and braided lines.

Standard Lines
Standard monofilament is widely available. Many very good lines fit the criteria described

A robust centre-pin reel is ideal for close-in float fishing, which is how Mark caught this double.

There are plenty of good quality lines for carp fishing in a variety of price brackets.

above at varying prices, but it is advisable to buy the best line you can afford. It is pointless spending a small fortune on the very best rods and reels and then be let down because you skimp on the quality of line. In any case, standard mono is relatively cheap, and is suitable for most carp-fishing methods. Compared to braid it is stretchy, with a typical stretch factor of around 10–20 per cent, although this is reduced somewhat in the most expensive lines, such as Shimano Technium.

The advantage of line stretch is that it gives an additional cushion when you are playing carp, something almost completely absent with braid. The disadvantage is that at very long range, over a hundred yards say, this stretch can make it difficult to set the hook. Monofilament sinks readily, but some monos sink more readily than others. Choose according to the method you intend fishing; for instance, you want a mono that sinks rapidly for long-range legering, and one that is more buoyant for up-in-the-water or surface bait tactics.

Good lines include Kryston Snyde, Daiwa Sensor, Maxima, Shimano Technium and ESP.

Braided Lines

Many carp anglers use braided lines for their thin diameter and non-stretch qualities, and because they are more inclined to float, a distinct advantage when fishing surface baits. The thin diameter also lends itself to long-range casting. A word of caution, though: braid makes no allowances for error, the lack of stretch meaning that the rod has to do all the work, absorbing all the shock of a fish making sudden, headlong runs. The lack of 'give' in a braided line can result in hook pulls and lost fish if the angler is taken by surprise. One of their advantages, however, is that they are considerably thinner in diameter for a given strength than monofilament lines. However, braided lines are best left until the angler has plenty of experience tucked under his belt.

There are, however, a few myths about braid, passed on by anglers who don't fully understand lines and their properties in water. It has been written by more than one well known carp angler that braid gives you instant bite indication due to its lack of stretch. This is simply not true,

Protect your finger with a special casting glove like this one from Gardner when using braid to cast long distances.

because a fish that pulls hard enough to start stretching mono is pulling hard enough to move a big lead and any indicator of reasonable weight. Also, any line follows its own curve through the water, and stretch, or lack of it, has no effect whatsoever on this happening. One hundred yards (90m) of mono or 100 yards of braid will travel through the water in exactly the same way when pulled by a fish, and stretch, or the lack of it, will not affect that. It's a somewhat different situation when quivertipping or fishing off the rod tip for other species, for braid will make a difference to the bite as the bend in the quivertip or rod is taken up.

Take care when putting effort into a long-range cast, as braid is thin enough to slice into your finger: use a finger stall or a neoprene glove. Bear in mind, too, that some clubs have banned braided main lines as they are considered to be much more likely than mono to tether carp following a breakage. Braided lines are considerably more expensive than monos, but usually last longer.

Fluorocarbon and Coated Fluorocarbon Lines

Few, if any, carp anglers use pure fluorocarbon lines as main lines, but reserve it for use as hooklinks and leger links. Fluorocarbon is stiffer and denser than nylon, and due to its refractive index being similar to that of water it is hard to see when submerged. Fluorocarbon, due to the extra stiffness, is very popular for stiff rigs, of which more in Chapter 7, Terminal Tackle and Rigs. Something of a compromise, and a much cheaper option than pure fluoro, are good quality nylon lines coated with fluorocarbon, such as Kryston's Krystonite, which you can use as main lines and are popular on very clear waters such as most gravel pits.

Shock Leaders

This chapter wouldn't be complete without mentioning shock leaders, for they form part of the main line when extreme distance casting, or when casting very heavy weights such as a loaded spod. Without a shock leader you would be taking a very dangerous risk, as a line breakage would mean there could be a rogue lead of 3oz (85g) or more flying through the air like a bullet, seriously injuring or even killing anyone who was unfortunate enough to be on the receiving end. At the very least a breakage would mean a carp could end up towing a heavy lead and a length of line around the lake.

A shock leader is a length of much stronger line knotted to the main line, long enough to hang up to 6ft (2m) from the rod tip with several turns remaining on the spool. An overall length of about 40ft (12m) is about right. Ideally, commercially available tapered leaders, with a breaking strain of 12lb minimum at the thin end and up to 45lb or more at the thick end, should be used as these will cast better, the thicker end absorbing the shock of casting and the thinner line tapering away and flying more easily off the spool and carrying the main line with it. As a rule of thumb you need 10lb of line strength for each ounce you're casting, thus 30lb for 3oz (85g), 60lb for 6oz (170g).

The knot that attaches the shock leader to the main line is of course vitally important. Not only should it be safe, it should also be as compact as possible so as to cause the least obstruction to line peeling over it on the spool and to its travel through the rod rings – and not least to prevent tethering a carp by allowing the terminal tackle to pass over it should a breakage occur. Some anglers use the double grinner but the Mahin knot is preferred by many anglers. A drop of superglue on the knot finishes it off and helps it slip through the rings more easily. An even better way is to form a covering of epoxy resin over the knot, shaping it so that it is tapered at both ends. This will give extra protection to the knot and allow it to slip more easily through the rings both in the cast and on the retrieval.

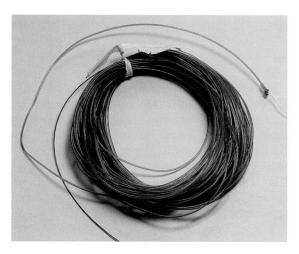

Shock leaders are essential when casting heavy weights to long distances.

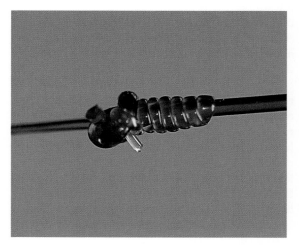

The right knot, like this Mahin knot, will help casting distance and ensure safety.

6 OTHER EQUIPMENT

Just how much equipment do you need? Because carp fishing dominates the UK coarse-fishing scene, there have been massive developments in every type of tackle item that you could possibly need, and probably a vast amount that you don't need. The danger, therefore, is to equip yourself so extensively that it is a major accomplishment just to get to your chosen swim, regardless of the distance from the car park; and once there, to find the prospect of moving such a daunting mountain of gear too much hassle to be worth the bother.

In short, less can sometimes be more, especially for short-session carping. The ability to travel light, yet sufficiently well equipped for every eventuality, is the mark of an experienced angler. It means that you have what you need, yet can move between swims quickly and efficiently, taking advantage of developing situations. For long-session angling it is a different matter altogether.

Landing Nets

The simplest option for a carp-fishing landing net is to buy a standard 42in (105cm) carp net with a standard 6ft (1.8m) handle. It will land any carp swimming in British waters, and elsewhere too, without compromise. However, if you're fishing a water where the carp rarely exceed about 20lb (9kg), and you want to move around from swim to swim, there is no reason why you shouldn't use a smaller 36in (90cm) net where the net mesh is deep enough to engulf a twenty-pounder. Thirty-six inch (90cm) spoon-type nets with a rigid frame are ideal where there is plenty of marginal weed or lilies, enabling you to push the net through the weed much more

easily than you could with the larger bow-string carp net. It is a fact, anyhow, that a 36in net is big enough to deal with most carp that swim in British waters, but when manoeuvrability is not necessary it is best to play safe with a bigger net – after all, you can net small fish with a big net, but you can't net some big fish with a small net.

Consider, too, whether the standard 6ft (1.8m) handle is adequate for your carp waters; are there, for instance, high banks, or do you need to reach beyond strong marginal weeds where a longer handle, or a handle with an adjustable length, might be better?

Another useful accessory for large carp landing nets is a net float, a foam collar that attaches to the top of the handle where the net frame is attached. This useful little gadget keeps the net afloat, taking the strain from your arm and preventing the net from sinking too deep when you're netting a fish.

Carp Care and Weighing Equipment

Unhooking Mats

If you have no intention of weighing or photographing a carp, there is no need even to lift it from the water, but instead unhook it while it lies in the landing net in the margins. If you do intend lifting it from the water, for whatever reason, then use an unhooking mat. Most carp fisheries insist on them, but apart from that it is good practice anyhow, for it is vital to protect the fish from hard gravel banks or anything else that could damage it. Even in long, soft grass there is always a chance that some angler who has fished the swim previously may have left something sharp in the grass. It is best to be sure, and the only way to be sure is to use an unhooking mat.

Unhooking mats vary from simple foam-filled mats to more complex inflatable ones that may have walls to hold an inch or two of water and a flap to cover the carp. Covering the eyes of any landed fish tends to quieten it down. Certainly, if you are likely to be landing big carp in the 20lb-plus (9kg) size on a regular basis then it is worth buying the best unhooking map you can find. Inflatable ones that have a raised rim are probably the best, having both the best cushioning properties as well as good protection against a lively carp sliding off the wet mat.

Always have a container of water at the side of the mat to keep the mat wet and to keep the carp wet.

Forceps and Disgorgers

The best tool for removing a sizeable hook from a carp's mouth is a small pair of forceps or long-nosed pliers; keep them handy by leaving them on the unhooking mat. Take care not to damage the hook knot when you grip the hook shank, and if in any doubt change the hook and hook link. A large plastic barrel-type disgorger will also prove useful at times, especially for the possibility, however rare, of a deep-hooked carp.

Klin-ik

Klin-ik and similar anti-bacterial medications made for treating fish are a good thing for treating the small puncture left by the hook and any other sores or wounds on carp. Some fisheries insist on its use. This, too, is best kept near to or on the unhooking mat.

Weigh Slings and Scales

It is possible to weigh carp in a landing net head, but it is much easier and kinder to the fish, and more accurate, to use a proper weigh sling made for the job. These have drain holes and are shaped to hold the fish safely and comfortably, and are ideal for carrying it back to the water for returning.

OPPOSITE: A standard 42in (105cm) landing net easily coped with this 26lb (11.7kg) carp caught by Mark.

ABOVE RIGHT: Keeping a container of water close by enables you to pour water over a landed carp to keep it wet and healthy.

RIGHT: Applying medication to a carp's mouth.

You will also need a set of scales whose maximum weight will exceed the weight of any fish you expect to catch. For most anglers in the UK a set of 40lb (18kg) Avon Dial Scales will do the job reliably for a modest cost. Or if you're one of those fortunate anglers fishing waters where the fish exceed 40lb, there are other dial scales that record even heavier weights. Another alternative is to get a set of digital scales, providing you carry a spare battery.

The correct way to weigh fish is to zero the scales to the empty weigh sling before weighing the fish.

Carp Sacks

Carp sacks were very popular at one time, being useful for retaining carp for short periods while you readied camera and weighing equipment, and especially at night when you wanted to get a daylight shot. But three things have happened to change the situation. One is digital cameras and their facility to be able to instantly check the quality of a photograph. The second reason is the spate of carp thefts brought about by the high price of big carp and anglers wanting to stock other waters illicitly, and the subsequent banning of the carp sack by angling clubs and syndicates. And finally the misuse of sacks by irresponsible anglers who retained carp for ridiculously long periods, didn't stake them out

Weighing a big carp is much easier using a purpose-made weigh sling.

Using a small pair of forceps makes light work of unhooking this 35lb (15.8kg) carp.

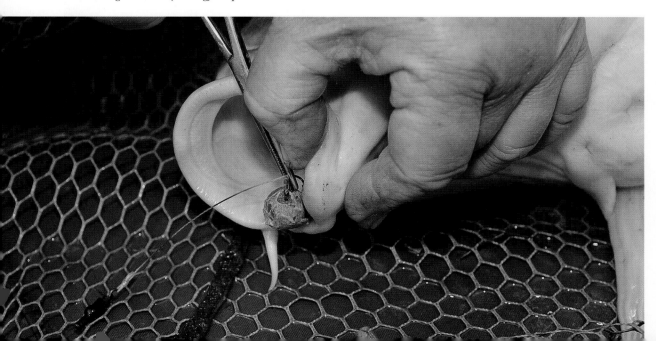

properly, and didn't retain them in shaded or deep enough water, often with the result that the carp died: another reason to ban them.

They are still a useful piece of kit when used responsibly, but it must be said that there are few reasons these days to sack a carp at all. If you do decide to buy one, make it a big one with lots of holes for good water flow, a safe zip or draw cord, and a long retention cord for securing it to the bank via tree or bank stick. Then make sure that you wet the sack before introducing the carp, that the water is at least twice the depth of the fish, and most importantly, make doubly sure the retaining cord is very firmly attached both to the sack and to the bank. The fish should have no chance whatsoever of being able to swim off whilst still in the sack. Keeping the carp for a couple of hours in the sack is more than enough.

Finally, when you retrieve the sack later, remember that the carp will have recovered all its strength and will tend to flap around a lot, both in your hands and on the unhooking mat. Be prepared for that and handle it firmly but carefully, and take your photograph as soon as it settles down, which it will do in a minute or so.

Bivvies

The modern angler has a marvellous choice when it comes to bivvies, from simple shelters to twin-skinned domes that can be erected in minutes and which are capable of withstanding anything the weather can throw at them. There are three basic types of bivvy, most of them available in two sizes, namely one-man or two-man: the shelter (with optional outer cover); the dome; and the twin-skinned dome – any other type is just a variation of one of these.

The Shelter

At its most basic, this is a glorified brolly with wings, or a simple pole-less brolly with an optional outer cover (with or without a door) that is thrown over it and pegged down. Without the optional outer cover it's a simple weather protector that's good enough for keeping out the wind and rain but offers only a little comfort in the way of warmth. The advantage of a shelter is that it is usually much easier to erect and a lot lighter to carry, making it ideal for short sessions, or day sessions as they're more popularly known.

This shelter is ideal for short sessions.

The Single-Skinned Dome

The dome offers better all-round protection from the wind and rain, and will stand up to heavy winds much better. It offers some warmth as well as total privacy. It usually has a door, and some have a storm porch.

The Twin-Skinned Dome

Two skins offer better protection and more warmth due to the enhanced insulation properties. They are much less inclined to sweat on the inside, which is one of the disadvantages of a single-skinned dome. Ideally you need a day shelter and a long-stay bivvy if you intend to do both. Some anglers compromise by having a day shelter and an optional outer skin to throw over it in more inclement weather or when on a long-stay session. Other considerations are how quickly and easily the bivvy can be erected. So to recap, when buying a bivvy you need to consider:

- Your budget.
- If you need protection for long or short stay, or both.

- If you plan to do 'overnighters' in winter.
- How big the swims are (some swims are too tight to take a large dome, especially a two-man one).
- If your long stays are likely to be for several days, because then you need to consider a two-man size to provide cover for the extra food, water and cooking equipment as well as yourself.
- How easy it is to erect, especially in a strong wind, and if there is likely to be someone there to help.
- Do you want a storm porch? (These are excellent when fishing with the door open and the wind is driving rain towards the front of the bivvy)
- Does it have a door that is not too low, so that you can get out of it in a hurry when the bite alarm goes off?
- The maximum height of most bivvies at the centre is around 5ft 6in (1.6m). If you're tall, avoid anything lower.
- Do you want your bedchair side to side (a wider bivvy) or front to back (a longer but narrower bivvy)?

For sessions longer than a day, a full-size bivvy (right) is a more comfortable option.

- If you choose a shelter, is there a groundsheet with it, or is one available as an optional extra?
- Does it have good ventilation so there is a good exchange of stale and fresh air?
- Does it have a mud flap at the door to help keep water and mud out?
- Are the pegs that come with it good enough, or will you have to pay more for decent ones?
- Do you need a rear door as well as a front door?
- Do you want windows in the doors?
- Do you want flaps over the windows?
- Do you want a mosquito mesh door for those summer nights?
- Does it have any loops or other facility inside where you can hang a torch or lamp?
- Does it have pockets where remote alarms and other bits and pieces can be stored?
- How heavy is it? Can you carry it as well as your other tackle, or will you have to make two or more journeys?
- Will the packed bivvy fit in your car without any problems?
- When the bivvy's been used a few times, will it still fit easily into the carry bag that it came in, or will you have to buy a bigger bag?
- Do the zips, toggles, D-rings and other fittings look strong and reliable?
- Can you get spare parts if you lose or break anything?

So there you have it, and there should be enough information for you to make a good choice of bivvy that will meet your exact requirements within the budget you have to spend.

Bivvy Accessories

There are plenty of accessories, but the handiest is a bivvy table and a bivvy lamp. The lamp is invaluable when night fishing, and the table helps you to keep things tidy and readily available.

Chairs and Bedchairs

Chairs

If you are going to be fishing just day sessions for a few hours then a folding chair should be ideal. There is a wide choice, and almost all of them fold up compactly, have some padding on the seat and back, and have adjustable legs. Some have arms for extra comfort. The weight of these chairs varies considerably; the very lightest are as little as 5lb (2.3kg), and the heaviest more than twice that. If you are getting to your swim using a barrow then it matters less, but if you need to carry it far then how much it weighs is important. The lightest of chairs are best for any roving fishing you may do.

Bedchairs

For overnight and longer sessions you will need a bedchair to lounge or sleep on. All of them convert between a chair and a bed to suit whatever type of relaxation you want at the time. For ultimate comfort choose a sprung, wide, padded one. Consider the weight factor if it has a bearing on where you fish and if you can use a barrow.

Sleeping Bags

For overnight and longer sessions a good quality sleeping bag is essential. Buy one with a TOG rating to suit the time of year you're likely to fish, or consider having two, one with a low TOG rating for summer and the other one with a high TOG rating for winter. Alternatively, buy one with a low TOG rating, and have an additional throw-over cover for winter. Another important point is to make sure the bag has burst-open zips for when you want to get out in a hurry to deal with a run, and that it has zips on both sides so that you can lie either way in the bivvy and still escape on the door side. For those who like to sleep in the open, some sleeping bags have showerproof outer skins to repel damp and dew. And don't forget a pillow!

Bait Delivery Gear

The obvious means of delivering bait to a swim is by hand, but this needs no explanation as its limitations are obvious. Other methods of delivering bait, such as spodding, PVA systems, the method feeder and the baitboat, are covered in other chapters. Just one word of caution: whichever method you use, from hand feeding to baitboat, accuracy is essential. The idea

A good catapult is ideal for firing boilies up to about 50 or 60 yards.

behind offering carp free feed is to attract them to the spot where your hookbait lies, to keep them in that area for as long as possible, and to give them a taste of the bait you have on the hook. So you can see that it is pointless doing all that in one spot when your hookbait lies in another. Even worse, and the biggest mistake many anglers make, is to spread free feed all over the place, in a wide area. That is worse than not baiting up at all, for it can divert the carp to several areas and possibly feed them to the point where, when they do come across your hookbait, they're too well fed to want it.

Catapults

At least one catapult is essential, but two or more is not overdoing it, because you will need one for particles, one for groundbait and one for boilies. It is worth carrying spare elastics for each catapult. Ensure that the boilies you fire out with a catapult are as perfectly round as you can get them, otherwise they'll fly off at a tangent and land just about anywhere other than where you want them to go.

Throwing Sticks

These are the carp angler's choice for delivering boilies to distant swims. They are round tubes in sizes to suit different boilie diameters. Make sure you use the correct size for the boilies you're using, neither too large a diameter nor too small. The tube has a curved end and the boilies spin out of the tube and can achieve incredible distances in experienced hands. The disadvantage with throwing sticks is that they're not easy to use until you've had a number of practice sessions, as it requires a certain wrist action to impart velocity with accuracy. Use with just a single boilie until you reach a certain proficiency, and then you can increase this to throwing up to four boilies at a time. When you master the stick you can bait a swim very quickly indeed.

A good idea is to wear a bait apron or a boilie bum bag so that you don't have to continually bend to fill the throwing stick, and so that you don't have to keep looking away from the target area and lose your feeding rhythm. Every two or three throws swill the stick out with lake water.

For propelling groundbait up to 50 yards, use a baiting spoon.

This will provide lubrication and prevent the boilies from sticking to the sides of the tube. As with using the catapult to fire boilies, make sure they're as round as possible and firm enough to withstand the pressure of being propelled from a throwing stick; some boilies are too soft for throwing stick use and will split in flight.

Hookbait Mounting Tackle

There are a number of small tools and accessories that are vital for mounting hookbaits. You need a hair needle to pull the hair through the bait, and a stop to go through the loop to hold the bait in position. And you need a drill for making holes in hard baits such as pellets so that you can get the needle through. Needles come in various sizes, but a short one is usual for mounting hookbaits, the longer ones more useful for making PVA stringers and PVA sticks. Hair needles have different tips to suit either mono or braid, and some have gates on the tip to prevent the loop from coming free when being pulled through. You can get very fine diameter needles for soft, more fragile baits.

An alternative to drilling a hard bait is to use a bait band, a tiny silicon elastic band that holds the hookbait to the hook. The best way of using a bait band is to attach one to the end of a very short hair (see picture sequence). Used like that, the band can go round the bait or be pulled through the hole in the bait and used like a conventional hair rig.

Yet another method of mounting hookbaits is to superglue them to the hair or direct to the hook.

Equipment for Creating and Storing Rigs

Braid scissors are essential, as ordinary ones make hard work of cutting braid. You can remove the outer skin of coated braids with your thumbnail, but a proprietary braid-stripping tool makes it much easier.

A knot puller helps to tighten knots and to test them before use without the danger of cutting your fingers with thin diameter line.

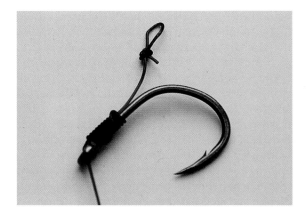

Rigging a bait band, step 1: tie a hair rig using the knotless knot and a small loop.

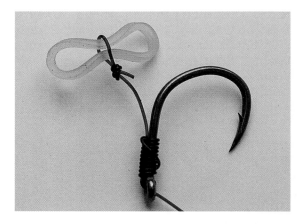

Rigging a bait band, step 2: insert a bait band halfway through the loop.

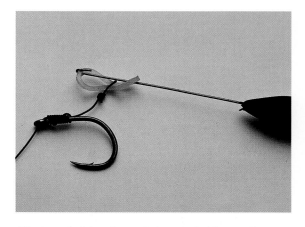

Rigging a bait band, step 3: insert a baiting needle through the bait band.

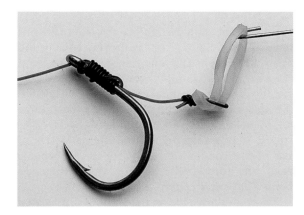

Rigging a bait band, step 4: use the baiting needle to pull the bait band back through itself.

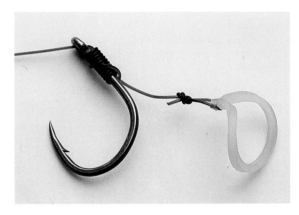

Rigging a bait band, step 5: tighten the bait band on itself so that it is securely attached to the loop of the short hair rig.

Stripping coated braid is simple using this Korda braid stripper. The Korda knot puller makes it easy to tighten knots without damaging the line or your fingers.

There are several storage devices for hook links. Take a look at them all and decide which one suits you best. Some are only good for short hook links.

Bite Detection and Rod Support

You need some kind of visual indicator to let you know what a carp is doing with your bait. A visual indicator, other than a swingtip, which is rarely used in carp fishing, hangs from the line between butt ring and reel or between the first two rod rings. It tells you if a carp is running away from you (by moving upwards as line is taken) or towards you (by dropping downwards as the line slackens) and how fast it's moving. Regardless of electronic bite alarms a visual indicator is essential.

Hangers

This does just what it says on the box; hangs from the line. It attaches to the line with a spring-loaded ball system, a gate, or some other kind of quick-release device. The other end of the hanger is anchored to the rod pod or bank stick with a cord or chain linkage. Usually the hanger has add-on weights. The more weight you add, the more resistance it offers the fish and the faster it will respond to fish that run towards you.

Swingers

This is more or less the same principle as the hanger but anchored to the rod pod or bank stick with a hinged arm. Weights can be slid along the arm, closer to the swinger head to offer more resistance and away from it to lessen resistance. The advantage of the swinger is that it won't move in a strong wind and give false bites.

Springers

Springers operate in the same way as swingers, except that instead of a hinged arm the arm is flexible. This can be tensioned so that it imparts a great deal of pull on the line and is especially useful for registering bites when fishing at extreme range, through taking up the slack line when a fish picks up the bait and moves the lead, but doesn't immediately move off.

Bite Alarms

Electronic bite alarms replace the front rod-rest head and have a device that the line runs round or on top of, either pulling an antenna to complete an electric contact, revolving a wheel that excites a magnetic field, or triggers vibrations through a sensitive reed. The result is an audible alarm along with an illuminated LED. The sound they transmit is most often a series of bleeps that run into one continuous tone when a carp hits top speed. Such coveted runs are known as 'one-toners'.

The vibration type is the most sophisticated and sensitive with the greatest array of adjustment in sensitivity, volume and tone. They usually have a built-in transmitter to trigger remote receivers. It goes without saying that they are the

LEFT: *Heavy hangers like these stainless-steel ones are effective in showing drop-back bites, especially at long range.*

BELOW: *Note the sophisticated alarms and bungee rubbers to stabilize the pod in high winds.*

most expensive. Most of the time you don't need all the features of the best, and a much cheaper alarm with nothing more than a volume control will suffice. Be wary, however, of some of the cheaper brands as they are not all waterproof and will eat batteries with a very expensive hunger.

Remote receivers are very good for having inside a bivvy when you're grabbing some sleep. You can turn down the alarm volume and have the remote on your bedchair side bivvy table. The remote will wake you, and the LED will tell you which rod is the lucky one with the run, so that you can dive out of the bivvy and know already which rod needs your attention. Remote receivers are very useful at night when you don't want to waken other anglers on the lake every time you get a run.

Always keep at least two spare batteries in your kit.

Rod Pods

Rod pods are very popular with carp anglers due to the ease with which you can quickly set them up ready to take up to four rods, and because they can be stood on any kind of ground, including gravel and even concrete. There are two basic types, with variations of each, the standard one having four extending legs at 45 degrees from the centre column, and the goal-post type that have four upright legs. The goal-post type is the most stable but takes longer to set up. There are two choices for added stability; a rod pod made from stainless steel where the sheer weight keeps it pinned down, or a lighter, perhaps aluminium rod pod, that you pin down with bungee elastics and bivvy pegs.

This relatively heavy stainless-steel pod is further stabilized by having the points of the legs pushed into the ground.

Bank Sticks

Although a rod pod is the first choice of most carp anglers, there will be times when you don't want all your rods stationed in the same spot when fishing different swims, with the lines projecting from them in a large arc, or even from side to side when margin fishing. It's often far better to separate the rods by fishing them from bank sticks, and be able to point each rod directly at the bait. However, such a set-up takes up more bank space, and you need to be sure that the landing net can be easily reached from each set-up, also that you have a clear run to each one from the bivvy. Alternatively, use two landing nets.

Some anglers insist on using bank sticks regardless of the ground conditions, and hammer them in when they arrive if the ground is hard. Not only is this detrimental to their own fishing, it does no favours to those anglers who are already there and have been set up and sat quietly for some considerable time. Be considerate and use a rod pod rather than a hammer where the ground is hard.

Butt Grips

Use back rod-rest heads – butt grips – that will grip the butt of your rods firmly. This will help to ensure that when you get a screaming run there is no risk of the rod sliding along the rod pod or bank stick set-up and being pulled in. This is especially true with the modern fashion for ultra-slim rod butts.

Luggage

Luggage is needed to transport your tackle items to the waterside. We can't do without it. But there are many luggage items that we can do without, although this will differ from one angler to another depending on his needs and the tackle he uses. The essential items are described below; as for the rest, your best bet is to visit a large tackle shop and see what's on offer, and then decide if you need it. Very often we buy things we want, rather than what we need, and there is a big difference, so beware! Each piece of extra luggage can increase weight and bulk in itself, so it is a good idea not to add luggage just for the sake of it.

Rucksacks, Holdalls and Other Bags and Boxes

The carp world seems split between large rucksacks and holdalls. Rucksacks are probably easier to carry on your back, whereas holdalls load more easily on to barrows and should give up their contents more easily. Whichever you choose you will quickly find that the amount of tackle you carry expands to fill the space available. What is essential, though, is that the luggage you buy is tough, hard-wearing, waterproof and practical. For instance, you will find that some useful plastic boxes – ideal for carrying hooks, leads and other minor tackle items – fit perfectly into the same company's holdalls. Integrated systems like this are worth checking out, because they enable your carp fishing to become better organized.

As well as the larger items of luggage, there is a massive range of smaller luggage items that range from reel cases, bait buckets, cool bags (essential in summer for freezer baits and your own food), weigh-scale holders and alarm cases through to larger items for holding cooking equipment and rod pods. Before you invest in every possible item under the sun, consider whether you actually need each and every one of them. Some tackle and accessories do need the best protection that you can find, digital cameras are an excellent case in point, but other gear can be stowed in larger luggage bags such as rucksacks or holdalls without additional protection.

Rod Holdalls

Modern carp-fishing rod holdalls provide excellent padded protection for carp rods with reels and terminal tackle already attached. For individual rods use a carp rod sleeve that also has padded protection for your reel. Although it is tempting to keep rods permanently set up this way for ease of getting set up each session, it is vital to ensure that the line, which is in danger of getting nicks and abrasions in transit, particularly when being loaded into vehicles and when the walk to the water includes paths through bramble bushes, remains undamaged. Periodically, whether you think it necessary or not, retackle the rods, discarding the last 5 yards of line. Other than that, ensure that the rod holdall you choose can indeed hold all the items you intend to take with you, and preferably has compartments that fasten to prevent anything from falling out.

Barrows

There are two basic types of carp barrow: those with one wheel, and those with two. Two-wheeled barrows are more stable and less likely to tip over, but one-wheeled barrows are easier to push over rough and muddy ground. So take a look at where you're most often going to use one, and let the terrain decide which barrow is best for you. Most have pneumatic wheels, and these are far superior to those with solid wheels.

Other things to look for are load capacity, ease of loading, and if it folds up compact enough to fit in your vehicle. It is best to take a look at the different ranges on offer from each manufacturer, and to decide which is best suited to your purposes. Don't forget to buy at least four bungee elastics to keep the load safely fastened to the barrow!

Head Torches

If you're going to night fish, or even just fish into darkness, you're going to need a torch, and a head torch is best so that you have both hands free for doing whatever you have to do where you need light and for walking off in darkness. The best and least expensive on batteries are the LED head torches, particularly those that can be switched between one or two to half a dozen or so LEDs, the dimmer light for baiting up and the brighter light for landing fish and packing away.

Enough gear for one day's fishing! This sturdy barrow is ideal for the job.

Cooking Equipment

Long-session angling means that you need cooking equipment for a hot drink and hot food, and one-burner or two-burner gas stoves fit the bill nicely. Other than that you need a spare gas cylinder, matches or a lighter, a kettle, a frying pan, a saucepan and a water container. And, of course, supplies of your favourite food and drink.

Cameras

There are few of us who don't want a photographic record of a particularly big fish we've caught, so carrying a camera has become rather an essential part of the carp angler's equipment. There is only one choice these days, and that is a digital camera. With a digital we can easily check on the monitor that we've got a good shot, and so can return the fish in a very short time. If you fish a lot on your own and are not likely to have someone around to take a shot for you, then the best digital cameras are those with a swivel monitor and a wireless remote control.

With such a camera you can set it up on a tripod or on a bank stick fitted with a camera adaptor, swivel the screen towards the unhooking mat, manually pre-focus the distance, and then it's an easy job to be able to see that you and the carp are in shot. With the carp on the unhooking mat and the camera set to take a ten-second delayed shot, press the shutter control, put the remote behind you, then pick up the carp and hold it nice and steady, just above the unhooking mat, ready for the shutter to be released. Two shots should do it, one most times. Now cover the carp and take a quick check on the monitor that you've got a good shot. Even if you have to take another shot, the fish needn't be out of the water for more than about three minutes, and if you keep it wet with that container of water you have handy, it will not come to any harm whatsoever.

Other Items

There are, of course, umpteen other tackle items that come under the 'luggage' umbrella, some of which will be useful, others a mere indulgence. No matter, take a look at what's out there and see if there is anything that you think will be useful to you.

Uncluttered and ready for action!

7 TERMINAL TACKLE AND RIGS

Hooks

The importance of using strong, reliable and sharp hooks cannot be overstated. As with most branches of angling, carp anglers are usually more concerned with rods, reels and all the other kit, yet that little length of bent metal at the end is crucial to attaching you, and keeping you attached, to a fish you may have waited a long, long time for. Poor quality or blunt hooks are far more likely to let you down than the latest and most expensive rods and reels! The best quality hooks of the right pattern conversant with the rig being used will ensure clean and secure hooking and holding power, with no chance of the hook pulling or straightening as the fish is played.

It is vital not only to know how to choose the right hook and understand what constitutes a good carp hook, but also to have total confidence in the hooks that you use. You will find that other anglers swear by a certain pattern yet find that you cannot get on with that pattern, or may have lost a good fish whilst using it and lost confidence in it.

Fortunately, the modern carp angler is well catered for, and a number of major manufacturers – including Korda, ESP, Owner, Fox, Korum, Drennan, Mustad and Gardner – market excellent hooks. Even so, check each hook you use very carefully, because even hooks from the same packet can vary and cost you fish. Pay particular attention to the hook point, making sure it's sharp and not turned over, and take a close look at the joint where the eye meets the shank; there should be no gap, and the end of the wire should have no sharp edges, as this is where breakages can occur, especially when using the knotless knot. The Korum seamless hooks are excellent in this respect as the eye and the shank are welded together, leaving no gap whatsoever to offer a sharp edge.

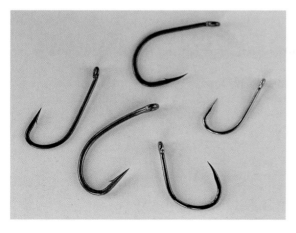

Amongst this selection of hooks there is the ideal hook for every carp-fishing situation.

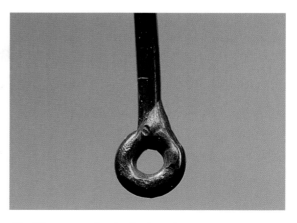

The Korum seamless hooks don't have the potential sharp trap where the eye meets the shank as in some conventional seamed hooks.

The design of carp hooks has evolved, and one of the most popular and successful is a short shank, wide-gape hook with a slightly inturned point and the eye turned slightly inwards. There are hooks with longer, curved shanks, but these are less versatile. At one time there was a fad for bent hook shanks, but these cause damage to the carp's mouth by turning during the playing of the fish and tearing tissue and are mostly banned – there is now no need to use them because we can emulate the hooking power of a bent hook by applying shrink tube to the shank of a conventional hook and extending it some little way up the line to offer the right curvature there. The arrangement is known as the 'line aligner' and will be explained in more detail further into this chapter.

Hooks do vary in strength. Most are perfectly suitable for general, open water carp fishing, but a lightweight hook may offer some advantages in bait presentation, especially when floater fishing or float fishing, providing you don't need excessive stopping power. But when it comes to hook-and-hold snag fishing you will need a stronger hook made from a heavier wire.

Similarly, the way the hook point is shaped, the quality of the steel and how it is sharpened all affect its ability to retain a sharp point. Nowadays most hooks are chemically sharpened to perfection, but this means the point is more vulnerable to being bent or blunted if they fall foul of gravel or any other hard object, and it is sensible practice to check the hook point before every cast. Runs are usually at a premium when fishing for big carp, and you can't afford to throw away the chance of converting every run into a fish on the bank through using a blunt or otherwise damaged hook.

Use a top-quality hook sharpener like this fine diamond file to touch up the point of your hook.

Choosing the Right Hook

One decision you need to make before choosing a hook pattern is whether or not you're going to use barbed or barbless. The debate over the pros and cons of barbed and barbless hooks is a never-ending one, with most clubs or managers of big-fish fisheries opting for you being able to make your own choice. Just a few insist on barbless, and even fewer insist on barbed. Make sure you check the rules before fishing, and then make your own considered choice if that has been left to you. Most carp anglers opt for a micro-barbed hook, which offers a fair compromise between hooking safety and fish conservation.

If you look at all the various patterns available and try to marry each pattern to a specific rig or situation, you'll just end up confused. And it's all completely unnecessary, as just one tried and tested pattern will suffice for almost all your carp-fishing needs. First, choose a hook of medium strength, short shank and with a slightly inturned point. This pattern is the most widely sold by all the manufacturers, and it wouldn't worry the majority of carp anglers if it were the only hook they could ever use. You can vary how the hook behaves according to the rig you use and the judicious use of shrink tube.

As for the size of hook, this will vary according to the size of bait you're using, including when hair-rigging, for a hook size that is not correct for the bait size will lead to missed runs through not hooking the fish in the first place, or through hook-pulls during the ensuing fight. Most often you will use a size 6 hook, as this is the most suitable size for 14mm to 18mm boilies. Use that as a starting point, and it's easy to judge what size of hook to use for boilies less than 14mm and greater than 18mm, and also easy enough to judge what size of hook you need for other baits of roughly the same size.

Weights, Lead Core and Other Terminal Tackle

Weights

Once the only specifically designed fishing weight that carp anglers used was the pear-shaped bomb, otherwise known as the Arlesey bomb; now, however, there is a wide variety of weights on the market. Some are flat for use over soft, perhaps silty bottoms, some are dumpy to offer maximum resistance in a bolt rig, some are knobbly to grip the slopes of gravel bars, and yet others are pointed and extremely streamlined for ultimate distance.

At about the same time as the Arlesey bomb was the only choice, a 2oz (56g) lead was considered to be really heavy, for in those days avoiding resistance in a rig was considered vital, and everyone fished as light as possible. But things change, and we now know that we can make resistance work for us rather than against us, and this has lead to increasingly heavy weights being used in carp fishing. A 2oz weight today is a little on the light side, with a 3oz (85g) weight more like the norm. There are now 4oz (113g) and 5oz (142g) leads on the market, and the whole range goes up in ½oz (14g) divisions.

It doesn't end there. We have pendulum-style leads, based on the original pear-shaped bomb with a swivel built into the narrow end, and we have in-line leads, with a hole through their length. Each has its pros and cons, which will be explained in the rigs section.

Furthermore, leads are now rarely left in their original colour, but are coloured and coated with various materials to blend in with different lake bottoms; you can also buy weights made from real pebbles (Stonze).

Lead Core

Lead core refers to a line that has an outer weave of fibres such as braid, and an inner core of lead wire. It is used for its property to sink and stay pinned to the bottom rather than, like some braids, lying in coils and rising from the bottom with the inherent risk of spooking wary carp that may touch it. It is built into some rigs, or used above the rig itself for up to 2 yards. It is also a very tough line that will cut through weed, and is extremely resistant to abrasion.

It is banned on some carp waters where careless anglers have used it and it has broken, leaving fish trailing a length of lead-core line that snags easily and is hard to get rid of.

ABOVE RIGHT: Lead core, seen in this rig, is useful for pinning down the line near your rig, but be aware that it is banned on many waters.

There are a wide selection of weights here: streamlined ones for long casting, dumpy ones for bolt effect, and some on safety clips.

Always, and that word cannot be emphasized enough when using lead core, *always* make sure that whatever rig you tie up, or in whichever way you use lead core, if a breakage occurs the fish can rid itself of it. In particular, make sure that swivel rings and other rings are large enough to ride over the joints between lead core and line, and that any knots you tie in it are not too bulky. Lead core offers distinct advantages when abrasion and weed is a problem, and when you want to be certain that your line lies flat on the bottom out of the way of wary carp, but none of that is worth it unless you take enough care to make it safe.

Other Terminal Tackle

There are lots of other smaller but none the less important items that make up various end tackles. Swivels are widely used, the most popular being the ordinary barrel swivel, most often used in size 8. This is also available with a larger ring at one end for use in running rigs. Another popular swivel is the ring swivel, or flexi swivel, which has a larger ring looped within the ring at one end, which is mainly used in pop-up rigs. Other odds and ends are various rings, both round and oval in different sizes, beads, link beads, silicon tube, rig tube, sleeves, lead clips and other bits that are no more than derivatives of the latter items.

Rigs

One of the most complex areas of carp fishing is deciding what rig to use, or it can be if you get into the mindset that catching carp is all about choosing the right rig. It isn't, of course, but it is an important part of the whole process. Simplicity though, is usually the key.

Carp anglers have devised literally scores of rigs that vary from the simplest to the extraordinarily complex. The truth is that most carp anglers, even the most successful, use very few rigs for their carp fishing. Once they have settled on a rig that works for them, in which they have total confidence, doesn't tangle, and on which they've caught a number of carp, then that's the one they stick to for the majority of their fishing. From time to time they may devise new rigs to while away the hours in the bivvy, but in most circumstances it is the original rigs, often with slight modifications, that are the best. Rig devising and making, however, is as much part of the enjoyment of carp fishing as is devising and tying flies in fly fishing. It doesn't have to be necessary to be enjoyable!

There is no universal rig that is the best. Some anglers favour rigs with in-line leads, others favour rigs with the lead on a safety clip, whilst others prefer a helicopter rig, some favour very

Graham concentrates on making rigs. Lager is optional!

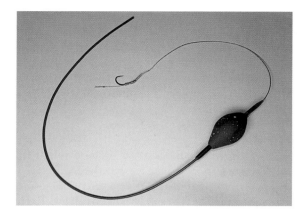

This simple semi-fixed rig with rig tube and in-line lead works well in most circumstances.

short hook links, others much longer ones. They can't all be right, or wrong for that matter. There is no doubt, too, that many anglers catch *in spite of* their rigs, rather than because of them.

As with all fishing, keeping it simple is the key to success. It is easy to overload a rig with lengths of tubing, beads, swivels, rings, lead core and other paraphernalia, each with some supposed function – yet the net result could be clumsy and counter-productive. Start with the necessities of a line, weight and hook, and only add those components that make a positive contribution to its effectiveness.

By working in this uncomplicated way, rigs can be seen to meet the needs for effective carping: that means a rig that presents a bait well enough to fool the carp. It means a rig that aids hooking the taking carp, and retaining that hook-hold throughout what may be a prolonged fight. It means a rig that does not spook carp, and one that does not tangle easily even when cast long distances. How well it casts does depend to a degree on the rig design. For distance work over 100 yards (90m) it is essential to get the rig design right, but at much shorter distances, such as 40 or 50 yards (36 or 45m), virtually any rig can be made to work. And much more carping is carried out at these modest distances than at ultra-long range.

The Basics of a Rig
The root of a carp rig is in essence a simple fixed or running leger rig. The basic running rig usually

consists of a pendulum weight stopped by a swivel and a buffer bead to which is attached a hook link. The basic fixed rig is much the same but the lead, which can be a pendulum or in-line type, is trapped in some way so that the line can't run through it. Add a hook link, and it is the variations around those basic components that can make or break the success of a rig: how big a weight should you use, what type of weight, what type of hook link, how long a hook link, what type of hook, how big a hook, how the hook/bait should be rigged … Endless questions and with no single answer. Yet by understanding the basic principles and the mechanics of carp rigs, the particular circumstances (casting distance, presence of weed or silt, need to attach PVA bags or stringers) and the bait being presented, it is easy to make uncomplicated, effective carp rigs.

A rig has several primary purposes:

• To present a hookbait that will fool a carp into taking it.
• To promote the secure hooking of the carp.
• To have sufficient casting weight to reach the swim.
• To enable the rig to be cast without tangling.
• To allow the bait to be presented for long enough for a carp to find it without it being tangled, hung up in weed or pulled out of position by wind or current.

Secondary considerations are:

• To avoid unwanted species ('nuisance fish'), crayfish and wildfowl.
• To introduce free feed to the swim.
• To allow the carp to be played without snagging on weed or sunken branches.
• To avoid scaring the carp.
• To withstand abrasion from underwater gravel bars or zebra mussels.

Understanding and Developing Rigs
Once you understand the basic principle of rigs, you can then modify existing rigs better to accomplish what you are trying to achieve regarding bait presentation. Furthermore, if you feel it necessary, or simply because you want to experiment, understanding the basic principles makes it easier for you to develop your own rigs.

Understanding the development of the hair and bolt rig gives you a great insight into the important basic principles. Without going too much into the history of these great developments, it is an advantage to know how they came about.

The Hair Rig

The most significant and radical development in carp fishing (indeed, as history shows, in most specialist fishing) is the hair rig, which was developed in the late 1970s by Lenny Middleton and first published in 1980. What led to its development was the fact that carp anglers realized that carp were taking hookbaits into their mouths, but rejecting them immediately they felt that suspicious difference between a loose offering and the one with a hook in it. The first move was to attach the bait with a human hair (hence the name 'hair rig') and this had two effects, the first being that the bait behaved a lot more like a loose offering in that it was free to move very slightly and thus didn't arouse as much initial suspicion.

Secondly, and what turned out to be the greatest advantage of all, was that the hook was left free to do its job. No longer was it masked with bait, and when the carp sucked the bait into its mouth, pulling the bait along with it, when it tried to blow it out again when it felt the hook, it could no longer do so with the same

certainty. The hook gained a hold as it was being ejected. Over the years carp anglers came to realize that it was the unfettered hook that was the hair rig's greatest advantage, and that a very fine hair was unnecessary. Today the hair is most often a simple continuation of the hook-length material.

The Bolt Rig

When carp were still targeted only on relatively small waters, the ultimate rig was the freeline rig, which is nothing more than a baited hook on the line. No weight whatsoever was involved. Each additional dram of weight was considered a move in the wrong direction, and anglers strived to reach even short distances because they were so reluctant to add additional weight to the terminal tackle.

But time moved on, and during the 1970s and 1980s, carp fishing continued to evolve. With the development and gradual maturing of gravel pits, carp fishing moved on from the traditional estate lakes and ponds, especially in areas such as Kent and the Colne Valley in Middlesex. Gravel pits are much bigger than traditional carp waters, often being many tens of acres. Carp anglers found that the bars and troughs of the gravel pits, created by gravel extraction, were invariably the hot-spots, and that many of them lay some considerable distance from the margins. Thus there was a greater need to cast

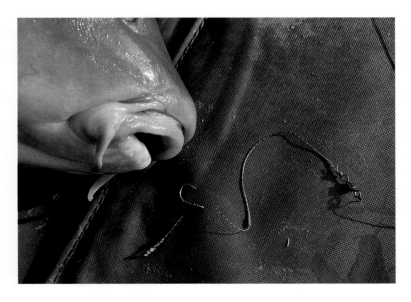

A simple hair rig, tied here with stripped-back coated braid, together with the boilie stop still in place.

longer distances, which meant more powerful rods (still in the era of glass fibre) and, of course, much heavier leads. The rigs were at first simple running Arlesey bombs, stopped by a leger stop or swivel. Despite using much heavier weights, the carp anglers found that they were hooking a higher proportion of runs than the 'strive for resistance-free bait presentation' logic of the time suggested.

Eventually they realized the implications of this – besides which, a few anglers were already experimenting with other means of offering resistance, and coming to the same conclusion. This author, Graham Marsden, was stuffing tapered foam bungs into the butt rings of his carp rods so that a running carp was running against resistance. The initial idea of this was to prevent hook pulls due to slack line falling off the open spool (this was before the days of the Baitrunner), but it soon became apparent that the initiative also led to more runs in the first place. At about the same time, Graham was experimenting with offering more resistance to big bream to convert more bites from that species into fish on the bank.

It eventually became clear that you could make resistance work *for* you rather than against you. Those who finally developed the ultimate bolt rig, the totally fixed lead (before the days when semi-fixed rigs were developed as a carp conservation measure), reasoned that when the carp picked up the hair-rigged bait and the hook pricked the carp's mouth when it tried to reject it, leading to it bolting off in fright, then the heavy, fixed lead would go a long way towards hooking the carp. Over time, to enhance the bolt-rig effect the weights became heavier, with 3–4oz (85–113g) leads being the norm rather than the exception, with these heavyweight rigs being used as much in the margins as they are at range. Anglers were now hooking carp cleanly yet securely in the bottom lip. Heavy weight had now become an integral part of the carp angler's terminal tackle, no longer to be shunned, but incorporated cleverly into rigs that converted tentative takes into full-blooded runs, and dubious hook holds into fish on the bank.

The Braided Line Hook Link

Another development was the braided line hook link. Again, there was plenty of serious thinking and experimentation taking place. Nylon monofilament in the heavier 12lb and 15lb strengths needed when fishing for big carp is relatively stiff. Conversely, braided line, which is a line made by braiding together a great many very fine fibres, is much more flexible and therefore allows the bait to behave more naturally. But using braid came at a price, it being more difficult to knot as it tends to self-strangle, and therefore some standard knots that worked well enough with monofilament are useless with braid. It was also very prone to tangling around the main line when cast, which led to the use of rig tube. The popular tucked half blood knot used to tie on hooks and swivels was replaced with the grinner and the palomar, until eventually the 'knotless knot' came about. More about knots later, but the knotless knot is very braid- and mono-friendly, and also incorporates the hair rig.

 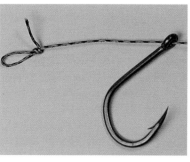 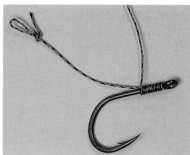

Start by stripping at least 7in (18cm) of the outer skin of the coated braid.

Make a loop, and pass line through the eye of the hook.

Trap line to the required hair length, and whip towards the bend of the hook for ten turns.

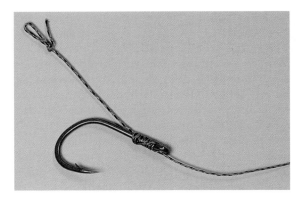

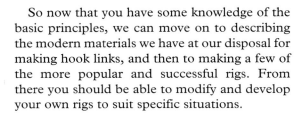

Take one turn around the whipping, and thread through the eye.

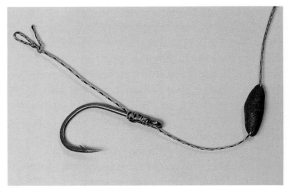

The peeled back point (2in (5cm) from the eye) makes an ideal place for tungsten putty when fishing a pop-up.

So now that you have some knowledge of the basic principles, we can move on to describing the modern materials we have at our disposal for making hook links, and then to making a few of the more popular and successful rigs. From there you should be able to modify and develop your own rigs to suit specific situations.

Hook Links

Kryston Advanced Angling were the first company to specifically make hook-link materials for carp anglers. Of course, it helped that Dave Chilton was a keen carp angler himself and knew exactly what carp anglers wanted. Today there is a vast array of materials, but they can be broken down into two categories with two variations in each: monofilaments, nylon and fluorocarbon; and braids, uncoated and coated.

Nylon Monofilaments

We have had nylon monofilament for years, and carp anglers mainly use it as a main line on the reel, although it was also used quite successfully as a hook link in the early years of carp fishing. A few carp anglers still use nylon mono as a hook link, mainly to offer a difference when trying to fool educated carp.

Fluorocarbon Monofilaments

Fluorocarbon mono is a fairly recent development. It was originated by the Japanese company Kureha in the 1990s with brands such as

Riverge and Seaguar. What makes fluoro different is the fact that it has a refractive index close to that of water, making it almost invisible under the surface. It is somewhat stiffer and denser than nylon mono, and sinks faster and lies flatter on the bottom better than nylon, making it very suitable for some of the carp rigs we use. Furthermore, it takes in less water when submerged, and is generally more durable than nylon.

Braided Lines

Braided lines are exactly what you would expect: a great number of extremely fine filaments braided together to form a relatively strong single filament. Their advantage over nylon and fluoro monos is their strength/diameter ratio, braid being much finer in diameter for a given strength. Because of this, braids are much more supple, making them less prone to detection by wary carp, and allowing baits to behave more naturally. Although there are many varieties of braid – sinking, floating, stiff, supple and so on – there are just two basic types: uncoated and coated. Coated braids have a type of plastic skin on them, which makes them stiffer, more durable to abrasion, and open to modifying by stripping some of the skin away.

Uncoated Braids
This is probably the most 'natural' material, in that it is soft and supple and less prone to detection when carp investigate baits. The negative aspect is that it is very prone to tangling around the main line when cast, necessitating the use of a

By preparing hook links you can quickly replace a hook link or hook.

length of rig tubing above the hook-link connection. In some instances it can be a little too supple, allowing the carp to play around with the hookbait without the hook pricking it, and making it bolt.

Coated Braids

This is now the most popular hook-link material with carp anglers. It offers all the advantages of the uncoated braid, but with more abrasion resistance, it tends to tangle less and, best of all, there is scope to strip off some of the skin to offer a short length of very supple braid right next to the hookbait, exactly where it matters most, whilst still retaining an element of stiffness where the skin remains to aid hooking power.

Stiff Links

The stiff link looked to be nothing more than a current fashion when it was first popularized in the nineties, but it has matured with time and become a successful and popular gambit. A stiff mono called Amnesia was the one to use, but since then heavy – 25lb and more – lengths of fluorocarbon are used. More about stiff rigs later.

Hook-Link Length

There is no ideal length: it depends on the rig and what you are trying to achieve with it. A standard length of about 9in (23cm) will probably work most of the time when using a bottom bait, but never hesitate to experiment with this length, both longer and shorter, when you suspect that carp are mouthing the bait but not being pricked by the hook. The Method feeder relies on much shorter hook links, the idea being that the carp attack the ball of groundbait, find

the hookbait, and take it thinking that it is just another free sample. The short link and heavy Method feeder provide the bolt effect. The hook link in this case may be as short as 3in (7.6cm), or a little longer when very big carp are the target. A popped-up bait will invariably need a short hook link of about 3in, but again, this can be varied to suit a specific situation; for example, if you're fishing in bottom weed that is a foot (30cm) deep, then a popped-up bait on a 14in (35cm) hook link makes sense.

Hook-link length is yet another of those things in fishing that just requires some investigation of the fishing environment, a taste of what's happening with the carp, and then the application of common sense and logic. How long a hook link needs to be is the same question as how long is a piece of string? It depends... .

Attaching the Bait to the Hook

Rarely these days do carp anglers use anything other than the knotless knot to attach a hook when a hair rig is being used, and it is a rare day indeed when a hair rig is not used. The main reason for this is that the knotless knot incorporates a hair rig in its design, and it is also one of the simplest knots to tie. It's called a knotless knot (or the no-knot) because it isn't actually tied off, but rather the coils of line whipping back up the shank and through the eye of the hook trap the line. It isn't totally necessary, but many anglers cover the coils with a short sleeve of silicon rig tube, or a longer length of shrink tube when incorporating the line aligner (*see* below). The knotless knot is suitable for all types of line; monofilament, braid and fluorocarbon.

Recommended Knots

Other than the knotless knot, the grinner and the palomar are amongst the most reliable. The Mahin knot is recommended for tying two lines together – that is, the main line to the shock leader. For joining the main line to lead core leaders, form a spliced loop in the lead core and use a grinner to tie the main line to the loop.

In tying your knotless knot and knots to rig rings, swivels and leads, take care to be consistent. Tighten the knots slowly and carefully, wetting the line with natural lubricant (spit!) before tightening, and ensuring that any coils in the knot are not overlapping. Knots are one of the few weaknesses between you and a hooked carp. Done properly your knots should not let you down. But if you damage the line in tying the knot, cut the end tags too short, or, especially in the case of braid and fluorocarbon, use the wrong knots, then knot failure is a strong possibility.

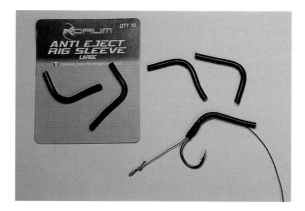

This is Jim Gibbinson's line aligner rig made from Korum's anti-eject rig sleeve, rather than shrink tube. Note that the line should emerge from a hole about 3mm from the end of the tube.

When tying the knotless knot it is possible to vary the length of the 'hair'. There is no exact formula for this due to variations in hook size and shape, and bait size and shape. In the early days, the hair was up to 3in (8cm) long, but this changed over the years as carp became educated and as anglers experimented with different lengths and with rigs that allow the hair to slide along the shank of the hook and with other variations on this theme. Today, the usual hair length is about 5–20mm from the hook. In tying the knotless knot, you need sample bait(s) to hand to get the length of the hair to your requirements. Of course, you won't always be using a single boilie; you might use two small boilies, or a boilie and a piece of artificial sweetcorn, and other variations, so make allowance for this.

Another advantage of the knotless knot hair rig is that it allows for mounting the boilie, or boilies, you intend using on the hair before the knotless knot is tied in order to get the exact hair

length you require. The bait can be removed once the rig has been tied. If you find you're missing runs or suffering from hook pulls, then seriously consider changing the length of the hair, either longer or shorter, as it is often the answer to such problems.

The Line Aligner

The line aligner, an innovation by Jim Gibbinson, is an excellent replacement for the very effective but non-carp-friendly bent hook rig. The line aligner emulates the bent hook rig by means of using a standard hook tied with the knotless knot hair rig, with the line from the hook eye threaded through a short length, about 1in, of rig tube that has been pushed on to the hook to just cover the coils of line. The trick is that the line emerges from the rig tube through a hole you've made in the rig tube about 3mm from the end.

In more recent times however, anglers are more inclined to use shrink tube to form that crucial bend in the tube. And the latest innovation is to use Korum's bent rig tube that already has the necessary bend in the tube.

Basic Rig Samples

The following are samples of some of the most popular, successful and pretty standard rigs used in carp fishing. Bear in mind that although there are scores of rigs used by carp anglers, when you examine them the great majority are just variations of these basic arrangements. One word of caution though before you begin to make any rig: make sure that every rig you tie is safe for the carp, and that it is not one of those we know as a 'death' or 'tether' rig. Always err on the side of caution, in that every rig should be built so that if the worst should happen and you suffer a breakage of the main line, the fish can escape without trailing a length of main line, plus the lead, and any other item of tackle you've used in the rig's construction, that could become attached to a snag and consequently tether the fish. Running leads should be able to slide off; fixed leads should be able to free themselves from the rig. The only thing a lost fish should be trailing is a short hook link, which it will be able to rid itself of in no time at all.

A word or two about the premise behind fixed and running rigs won't go amiss here. In theory at least, the fixed or semi-fixed lead provides a bolt effect due to that moment when a carp takes the bait and feels the lead, due to the line not being able to run through the lead. Conversely, in theory the running lead allows the carp complete freedom to take the bait without feeling the lead. In practice, however, in both instances the carp will feel the lead unless it happens to take the bait so that the line is being pulled through the lead, or the swivel, in a straight line so that

no friction is involved. If the carp takes the bait at an acute angle to the lead, then the running lead will probably be felt almost as much as a fixed or semi-fixed lead. Fishing a running lead with a very slack line negates the friction to some extent. Nevertheless, the one great advantage of running rigs, providing there are no huge knots or other impediments on the line, is that they are the safest rigs you can use.

Note that although there are descriptions of each rig, the photographs best illustrate how to tie them.

Basic Bolt Rig with Safety Clip

This is probably the rig most used by carp anglers. It uses a semi-fixed lead to offer the bolt effect, but a safety clip to ensure that the lead can pull free should any breakage occur. Use it with a length of tubing a few inches longer than the length of the hook link or with lead core.

The Running or Semi-Fixed In-Line Rig

Rigs don't come much more simple than this one, which is just the main line threaded through a length of rig tube and then through an inline lead and then tied to a swivel. The tube is plugged into the lead at one end via a tapered tail rubber and the swivel plugged into the other end of the lead, the hook link tied to the other end of the swivel. This very simple rig will catch carp on most waters, most of the time. If you want the

The lead in this semi-fixed rig uses a safety clip.

rig to be more of a running rig you put a bead on the end of the line before you tie it to a swivel. For a more abrasion-resistant rig, and one that will lie more tightly to the bottom, dispose of the rig tube and tie the main line to a length of lead core line, then thread the lead core through the lead, remove some of the inner lead core and tie the outer braid to the swivel.

The Running or Semi-Fixed Pendulum Lead Rig

Again, this is a simple rig. Tie in a length of lead core, or slide a length of rig tube on to the main line, ensuring it is longer than the hook link. Now slide on a pendulum lead fitted with a large diameter run ring, ensuring that the ring of the swivel is big enough to pass over the knot where the lead core is attached to the main line. Slip on a buffer bead and tie the line or the lead core to a swivel.

More Advanced Rigs

The simple rigs described so far – running, in-line lead and semi-fixed lead – are adequate for the vast majority of carp fishing. Despite this, there is a tendency to invent rigs for all sorts of imagined problems, giving rise to ever more complex rigs that do more to please anglers than they do to put more fish on the bank. These complex rigs are often less efficient than the simple rigs, despite claims to the contrary. There are some more advanced rigs, however, that can be useful in the right circumstances, which are described here.

Three factors come to mind that demand a different approach. These are the need to cast long distances, to overcome silty (or, colloquially, 'chod' or 'choddy') bottoms, and to cope with weedy conditions – typically many strands of Canadian pond weed. In all cases it is vital to keep the rigs as simple and uncluttered as possible, always considering whether the addition of yet another component to the rig is actually making it more effective.

The Helicopter Rig

The helicopter rig gets its name from the fact that the hook link can spin around like a helicopter

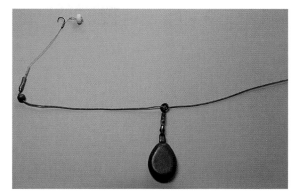

This simple running rig, shown here with lead core, is ideal for most short-range carp fishing.

rotor when the rig is in flight. It was originally designed as a tangle-free rig, especially when casting long distances, for which it is ideally suited due to the lead being on the end of the line rather than above the hook link. You can use lead core to tie up the rig, but this isn't mandatory.

Simple pendulum lead, used in various rigs.

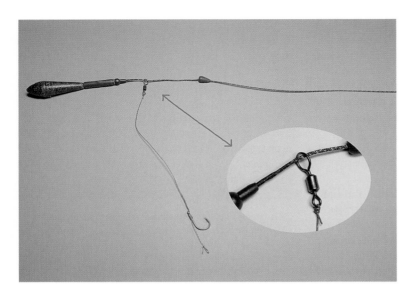

Use the helicopter rig to avoid tangles when casting to long range.

BELOW: Checking that the marker float is in the right position prior to spodding in the feed.

The simplest helicopter rig has the hook link between two tight-fitting beads with one or two silicon stops above the uppermost bead to prevent it from slipping when in flight. You can vary the distance between the two beads to allow the hook link to slide freely between them, or trap the hook link between the two beads, leaving only enough of a gap to allow the hook link to spin.

The Chod Rig

The chod rig is so named in that it is designed to overcome deep silt that is colloquially named 'chod'. In reality it is no more than a modified helicopter rig with a shorter hook link, usually fluoro for stiffness, of around 3in (8cm), and with a much greater distance between the beads to allow for the depth of silt. The rig is usually built on lead core, which is preferable but isn't totally necessary. If you don't use lead core then ensure you counterbalance the hook link at the swivel end with a blob of heavy metal putty. The bait used is a pop-up, either a buoyant boilie or a buoyant imitation bait.

There are many complex variants of this rig, including ones that try to take the free movement of the bait to extremes, with the hair passing back through the hook eye to hold a rig ring to which the bait is attached. This simple version described works equally well if you use a bait with sufficient buoyancy.

The Confidence Rig

Again, this uncomplicated rig is nothing more than a slight modification of the running rig. The difference is that you thread a tight bead on to the lead core, or use a couple of silicon stops on mono, several inches or even a foot or more above the swivel stop. The idea is that the carp can take the bait with confidence those several inches or more before the swivel ring on the lead bangs up against the bead or stops and applies the bolt effect.

ABOVE RIGHT: The confidence rig is often used when carp are being particularly wary of resistance.

Use the chod rig when fishing over silt.

The Weed or Rotten Bottom Rig

The weed rig is similar in some ways to the chod rig, but is designed to give good bait presentation but safe fishing in dense weed. The principal difference is that you attach the lead to a length of about 2ft (60cm) – depending on the depth of weed – of 4lb monofilament, which is attached, via a ring or swivel, to a yard or so of de-cored lead core (which is quite buoyant but abrasion resistant). Due to the 'rotten bottom', the maximum weight of lead you can use is about an ounce, but you'll get a little more grip if you use a gripper lead. As with the chod rig, use a pop-up boilie or other buoyant bait on a short fluorocarbon hook link of just 2–3in (5–8cm). This is prevented from flying off the de-cored lead core by a non-slip (but not fixed) rubber bead close to the join between the main line and de-cored lead core. Critically, balance the pop-up with a blob of tungsten putty around the swivel.

The idea with this rig is that although the lead will sink down into the weed, the bait should remain clear of it. If the lead gets caught up in the weed, then the use of a 'rotten bottom' will enable you to break free to land the carp. It is restricted to ranges of about 40 yards due to the necessary light leger weight.

This 30lb (16kg) plus carp fell to a simple in-line rig.

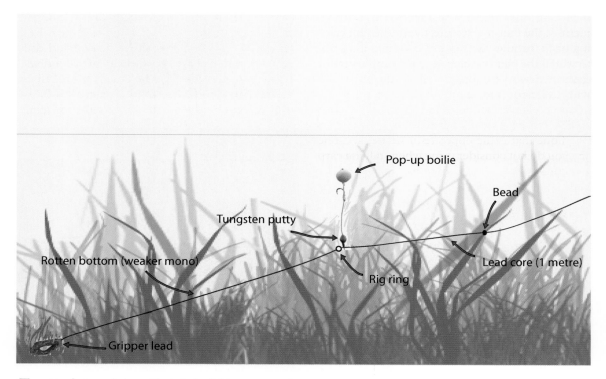

The rotten bottom rig is an ideal rig for fishing over weed.

8 THE METHOD, HIDING THE LINE AND OTHER THOUGHTS

There is more than one way to catch a carp, and this chapter will cover those methods that don't quite fit into the usual carp-fishing doctrine. It will also expand on some of the various techniques and 'edges' that are not always necessary, but when used in the right circumstances can make the difference between success and failure. Always remember though, that the trick is not just knowing about different techniques, it is also about knowing when to apply them, or when to apply one and not another.

Method Fishing

Method fishing is a widely used technique invented by a match angler and used by match anglers fishing for smaller carp in commercial fisheries where the fish are plentiful and almost always hungry, to the point where they have to compete with each other, and other species, for food. It has been adapted by carp anglers but is a technique that is the opposite of subtle, and one that you do not consider using when stalking carp and employing the 'softly, softly' approach. The Method is, of course, used to catch various species of big fish, not just carp, and in the right circumstances can be a deadly technique.

The Basic Rig

The Method is made up of a Method feeder – the popular ones are made by Fox, Korum or Korda – and a short hook link, often not more than 3in (8cm) long, though where big carp are expected it could be as much as 6in (15cm). The feeder, which is most often a three-finned device to hold the groundbait, is fished in line, the main line running through the feeder and a swivel tied to the end. The swivel is then plugged into the rubber grommet built into the end of the feeder, making the set-up a semi-fixed bolt rig, fixed sufficiently so that the bolt effect can operate, but safe because the swivel can be 'unplugged' should a breakage occur. You can, if you wish, include about 12in (30cm) of anti-tangle tube above the feeder to be certain that tangling will not occur when casting, especially when using a longer than average hook link; with short hook links, however, this is not usually necessary.

Hook Links and Hookbaits

The usual short hook link associated with Method fishing makes a popped-up bait an ideal choice, even more so when the hookbait is buried in the ball of bait: when the ball is broken by a foraging carp, the hookbait is released and rises to hover enticingly above the heap of groundbait. It follows that a stiff hook link made from 15lb or heavier fluoro, attached to the feeder via a Flexiring swivel to enhance the hinge effect, is going to be the ideal hook-link material.

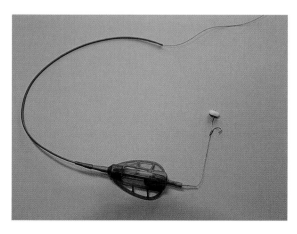

This is the basic Method rig: simple, safe and effective.

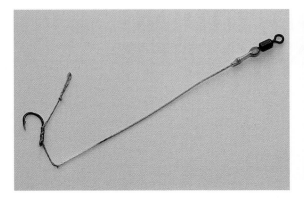

The Method hook link is short, and ready to prick into a fish that lifts the bait just a few inches.

Carp rods need to be on the heavy side to cast loaded Method feeders any distance.

As well as pop-up boilies, buoyant artificial baits such as sweetcorn make excellent hookbaits for the method. When non-buoyant baits are used – and any of the usual carp baits can be used with a Method feeder – any of the popular hook-link materials – braid, skinned braid and mono – can be used. You don't need anything special for Method fishing where hooks are concerned, just match them to the size and type of bait being used. The same applies regarding hair length.

How the Method Works

The principle behind the rig is to present a ball of groundbait that has a hookbait hidden within it, or lying alongside it. The groundbait, which can be laced with hookbait samples, or pieces of it – namely crumbled boilies – is moulded around the Method feeder. The hookbait is fished as normal on a hair rig, and you can leave it to hang free, or bury it in the ball of groundbait. The idea is for a carp to come along, find the ball of groundbait, and attack it to break it up; as it breaks it up it finds the sausage (the bait) on the plate of beans (the groundbait) and thinks, 'OK, I'll have some of that!' and takes the hookbait – and due to the short hook link, immediately gets pricked by the hook, which causes it to bolt. The Method feeder is heavy enough, even when free of groundbait, to go some way towards pulling the hook home.

To work at its best the loaded Method feeder should be cast often, and is ideally suited to prolific 'runs' waters, typically fisheries such as

Drayton Reservoir in Northamptonshire, where a day session is expected to produce a number of runs. Over several hours it can be cast regularly to build a swim and even create a hot-spot. For the sort of water where runs are few and far between and the carp big and wary, then it is probably not so ideal as it relies at least in part on the hungry carp responding to the 'banging of the dinner gong' effect of regular casting. The Method *is* used for large carp where the feeder is cast and left for longer than would be normal when Method fishing, but many of its advantages are lost due to infrequent casting.

Method fishing for carp is generally used at shorter ranges than other methods. The weight of a loaded Method feeder can vary depending upon the size of feeder used, but even using conventional carp gear its range is restricted to about 80 yards (73m), and it is advisable to use a shock leader, as the heavy weight and force required to cast a loaded Method feeder puts the line above it under considerable strain. Unloaded Method feeders weigh 2–3oz (56–85g) and up to 5oz (140g) when loaded, which means that a rod with a 3lb test curve is going to be the lightest rod you can safely use, with a 3½lb TC rod even better when casting to the longer distances.

The Method works best when you are targeting a prolific carp water where the carp have to compete for food and where it pays to cast frequently – and accurately – to the same spot throughout the session. Casting regularly can be as frequent as every ten minutes, or with longer intervals up to half an hour. Leave it much longer and you lose the effectiveness of the technique, which relies on the constant casting to build a swim that has sufficient food attraction and carp-feeding activity to get the carp feeding confidently.

Having established a rhythm of casting, stick to it and be patient that the carp will find your bait. Don't lose heart after an hour and stop casting; keep at it, and the Method will work. Unless, of course, you are targeting very big carp, and taking your chances that one will find your Method-presented bait that has lain there for a much longer length of time. In that case there may be a better way than the Method to present both feed and hookbait, and you should consider other options as well as the Method according to where you are fishing and the size of the fish you are targeting.

The Method Mix

As the Method has evolved from its inception in the nineties, the thinking around the best type of groundbait to use with it has changed, too. Originally the groundbait was a sticky mix, perhaps boosted with fish meal. The target fish for the Method were small carp in heavily stocked match waters. But as time went by it was adopted by carp anglers targeting bigger carp, and the thinking on groundbait changed. There now seem to be three options to choose from: the main one is a very fishmeal-rich proprietary groundbait usually labelled as such – 'Method Mix'. Another, and more economical option, has the dog food Vitalin, a food-rich sticky mixture as its base mix. And the third option is to use dampened pellets. What they all have in common, or should have, is stickiness, having the ability to adhere to the Method feeder while the feeder is in flight, and to remain on the feeder when it hits the surface and until it reaches bottom where it will slowly break up, or be broken up, by hungry carp.

A double-figure carp falls to a boilie presented on the Method.

This Method mix is a typical blend of food particles and a binding base mix that will quickly break down.

Vitalin dog food is an excellent and cheap Method groundbait.

Proprietary Method Mixes

These come in various forms, from fishmeal and breadcrumb-based mixes and various other ingredients such as crushed tiger nuts, peanut meal, crushed seeds, ground pellets, plus other attractors, many of which are 'secret' to the manufacturer and usually the most expensive. As with any groundbait, it pays to add water to the mix until it's a little wetter than you want it, and then allow it to soak for at least 15 minutes, preferably longer. Then adjust it by adding a little more dry mix. Finally, add such items as dry pellets, sweetcorn, hempseed, and crushed and whole boilies.

Vitalin-Based Method Mix

Vitalin dog food has long been used as a carp groundbait, and if mixed correctly it makes a superb Method mix. Vitalin contains cooked wheat, cooked sweetcorn, meat and marrowbone, soya, cooked barley, vitamins and minerals, so you can see that it is a protein-rich food that's not only good for dogs, but fish too! Vitalin is best mixed the night before you use it, or with hot water if you mix it on the day; only that way will you end up with a mix that will stick to the Method feeder. Be sure to mix thoroughly, preferably in a wide bowl where each of the flakes receives an equal amount of water. Add other ingredients, such as dry pellets, sweetcorn, hempseed, crushed and whole boilies, mashed tinned tuna or scalded maggots just before you use it.

Dampened Pellets

Any pellet will do, trout, halibut and coarse, but the smaller the pellets the better they stick to the Method feeder. Pellets can be given a quick soak in hot water, pouring it off immediately after a quick stir, or with cold water and left to soak at the rate of one minute per millimetre size of pellet – thus 4mm pellets are soaked for 4 minutes. That's the rule of thumb, but there is a variation in the soak time required for different pellet types, so be prepared to adjust the soaking time a little. Groundbait or crushed dry pellets can be added to adjust a soaking that is a little too wet, or a little water added to a too dry soaking.

With all three options you can add a flavour or oil to the water you use to mix it. And don't

---

Having the Edge

Here's a tip that will give you a little 'edge': when you mould the groundbait around the feeder, mould it so that it carries about twice as much feed on one side than it does on the other. Now bury the hookbait on the opposite side of this extra bulge of feed. The whole package will now be heavier on one side, and will ensure that the feeder lands this heavy side down with the hookbait on the upper side, free to fall off it, rise from it, and open to attack from the carp. If you bury the bait in an evenly packed feeder and the feeder happens to land bait-side down, it could take much longer for the bait to become exposed enough to be taken by the carp, or it could end up trapped between two of the fins and hidden from the carp. At least one manufacturer now makes Method feeders with the lead weight on one fin, which ensures it lands weight down; so be sure to bury the hookbait on the opposite side.

---

forget, having got your mix to the right consistency, cover it to prevent it drying out in the sun or getting wetter in the rain.

In addition to the feed introduced via the Method feeder it is a good idea to put additional feed into the swim using a catapult for the longer range swims, or a baiting spoon for the closer ones. This will attract the carp into your baited area and help them to home in on the hotspot you're creating with your Method feeder. But be careful you don't overdo it, especially on cold days when the carp are less likely to feed with any great appetite.

Hiding the Line

Most standard carping is practised with a tight line between terminal tackle and rod tip. This has some advantages in that the resistance at the rod enhances the bolt effect of the rig, and bite detection is a blurring run as the carp bolts away at high speed. If the carp bolts towards you, the swinger-type indicator or hanger type, which should be heavy and set close to the rod, will drop rapidly, taking up the slack line. The disadvantage of tight-line fishing is that the line comes up at an angle from the terminal tackle right to the rod tip, so any carp swimming and hopefully feeding near the rig will foul this rising line and possibly scare the carp away from the baited area.

There is one side to the debate that suggests it doesn't matter, that a carp may feel the line but not spook, since they must be brushing against seen and unseen objects in a lake quite frequently, and there is no reason to believe that brushing against a line will cause them any more alarm than brushing against, for instance, a weed stem. That said, the wise carp angler will err on the side of caution and ensure as much as he possibly can that the carp don't brush against his line; there is no point in taking any chances when you don't need to.

However, line fouling, or 'line bites' as we also know them, are prevented in several ways, and they all involve adding extra items to the tackle, which we can well do without unless absolutely necessary. It depends upon several factors: at short range your line will come up from the lead at a steeper angle than at very long range, where the sheer weight of the line will cause it to droop and possibly feel quite slack to a fish that may brush against it. In prolific 'easy' waters it may not matter too much as the urge to feed may be stronger than the urge to take flight. And finally, if you are using braided main line that can tend to float, some options may not apply; slack-lining for instance, but more of that later.

So the first move is to use a main line that is noted for its density and tendency to sink; fluoro-carbon is the best, but is far too expensive and stiff for use as a main line. Some anglers use a fluoro-carbon-coated line, but this isn't the same thing at all, which is why it's no more expensive than an ordinary mono, and it is certainly no more dense than ordinary mono, although it does have a little of the true fluoro's less visible properties.

Lead Core and Fluorocarbon Leaders

In most situations it is enough to pin the line down near to where carp activity is most likely to take place, and that, of course, is around the hookbait and baited area. We can do this to a degree with a 7ft (2m) lead core leader that will lie hard on the bottom, and has the added advantage of being stronger and more abrasion-resistant when fishing close to snags or weeds. Another option is to use a fluorocarbon mono leader of around 25lb break-ing strain, which is also heavy and dense enough to lie flat, perhaps not as much as the lead core leader, but at least the fluorocarbon line has the added advantage of not being as visible.

In either case it is important not to tighten up too much or we'll just lift the leader off the bot-tom anyway and be right back where we started. Following casting and just tightening enough to the terminal tackle to sink the line, pull a few metres of line off the spool to create some slack. This isn't the full Monty slack-line method, but it does allow the leader to lie flat.

A lead core leader is one way to pin the line to the bottom near the rig. It is shown here with a confidence rig and lead core.

Backleading

There are three types of backlead; the common one, via a split ring or clip, is hooked over the main line after casting. Captive backleads are much the same thing, but are anchored, via a cord, to the rod pod or rod rest for retrieval. And finally there are flying backleads, which are free running on the main line and an integral part of the set-up. Both conventional and captive backleads, weighing from about ½oz (15g) to as much as 4oz (113g), are hooked over the main line via a split ring or clip just outside the rod. You then lift the rod so that the backlead slides down your line and into the water. The higher you lift the rod and line out of the water, the further the backlead will slide towards the terminal tackle. The usual distance is up to two rod lengths out when fishing at long range, depending on the depth of the margins, or right in the margins if fishing at short range.

The flying backlead is a bored bullet-shaped lead that is convex at the thick end, or a bell-shaped lead that weighs about ¼oz (7g). This is threaded on to the line before you attach the terminal rig, making sure that the backlead won't jam on the end tackle and that it runs freely. The flying backlead works via air pressure, so when you cast, the backlead flies up the line and helps pin the line to the bottom. Again, you should avoid tightening up so much that you lift the flying backlead off the bottom.

Slack Lining

The true slack-line method is not the most popular of methods for the simple reason that many lack confidence in it, thinking that they will miss a percentage of runs due to its lack of sensitivity. Also, many anglers believe that they're slack-lining just by not tightening up to the end tackle. But this is a fallacy, because you have to go to greater lengths than that to ensure the main line from rod to terminal tackle is truly slack and offering no resistance.

It is set up with a heavy, up to 6oz (170g) free-running weight, using a large-bore run-ring. A dense, sinking main line should be used (making braid a poor choice), and the line at the terminal tackle end pinned down with a length of lead core and a flying backlead to pin the line to the bottom close to the rod. Following casting, the rod is placed on the rod pod, the indicator attached and allowed to fall to its lowest position, and line is gradually stripped from the reel as the indicator continues to rise and fall until the line has sunk to its full extent.

The theory is to offer a main line that is totally sunk, and lying slack on the bottom, with no chance of the carp being spooked by touching any part of it. It is also a rig that is the complete opposite of the bolt rig, a set-up where educated carp won't feel anything when they pick up the bait. The idea is that the heavy weight won't move when the carp picks up the bait, and the

Captive backleads are pegged to the bank via a length of cord, ensuring you don't lose them.

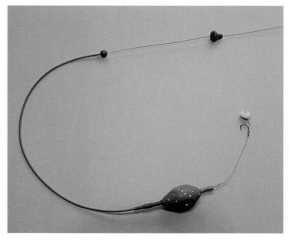

Flying backleads, as the name suggests, fly up the line during a cast and pin the line to the bottom.

A conventional backlead, used like a captive backlead but not pegged to the bank.

An ultra-light bobbin is only suitable at very short range or when slack-line fishing.

fish won't feel the weight due to this completely slack line being able to run freely through the large-bore run-ring.

It sounds great in theory, but many believe that this is a rig that works in spite of its properties rather than because of them, but it is offered in this book for you to try for yourself and draw your own conclusions. If it works for you and gives you confidence, then that's all that matters. If it doesn't make any difference to your catches, then revert to a simpler set-up.

Runs, Bites and Bleeps

A 'bite' in carp fishing is most often referred to as a 'run', for the simple reason that most 'bites' from carp are blistering runs that take several yards of line from a free-spool reel before the angler lifts the rod to complete the hooking process. There are times, however, and during the cold winter months is one of them, when the carp are so lethargic they hardly move at all after taking the bait. The same thing sometimes happens when very wary, suspicious carp are so hungry they can't resist taking the bait, but are taking it, or tasting it, so tentatively they're hardly daring to move. The result could be a single bleep on your bite alarm followed by a deathly silence, although the indicator may not have fallen back to its original position, which is often a clear indication that the carp is hanging on to the bait.

The only way you are going to convert that bite into a hooked fish, assuming you can't offer the bait on a better self-hooking rig, is to strike at it and ignore your natural instinct to wait for the full-blooded run or the inclination to assume it is a line bite.

Once you have reached the conclusion that the single bleeps are indeed feeding carp, rather than the attentions of unwanted species ('nuisance fish'), and that the self-hooking rigs are not working, the next move is to try to exaggerate the single bleep into something more positive, and a very free-running rig is probably the answer. Tackle up with a pendulum lead on a short link, which has a large-bore run-ring running on the main line. Lead core can be used to ensure it's all pinned down. Make sure the rod is lined up exactly with the baited area to cut out as much friction in the rod rings as possible, and cast in, tighten up, and set the lightest indicator you can get away with on a loop of line that hangs just a few inches from the rod. Now sit by the rod with the free spool of the reel locked, and be prepared to strike as soon as the indicator lifts. If your suspicions are correct, you'll hook the carp – if not, then you've lost nothing anyway. It's much better to try something like this than always to assume single bleeps are line bites or something else other than cautious carp taking the bait. Very often the biggest, most wary carp are responsible for the most innocuous indications.

Setting the indicators.

Problems Perceived rather than Real

Very often we anglers see problems where none exist. It is our natural tendency to try different baits and rigs following a prolonged blank period, particularly when that blank period stretches over several sessions, even lasting for weeks. There is nothing at all wrong with that, for a change of bait or rig, or swim, could be just the answer. Very often though, there is nothing you can do to remedy the situation, for every water, especially big-fish waters, go through spells when the fish just don't feed, or feed on some natural food creature to the exclusion of all else.

It's always a good idea, when you've tried several changes without any improvement, to find out if other anglers on the lake are suffering the same way. If any of them are still catching successfully then you know there are changes you can make that will put fish in your net again. If none of them are, and haven't been for a similar length of time as yourself, then you can safely assume the fish are going through a non-feeding spell for one reason or another.

The trouble is, if we're not aware of the possibility of a 'natural' fallow period, we can work ourselves into a really worried state trying different methods and baits, and then arrive at a completely false conclusion. For instance, we may have tried everything until we end up with a rig that resembles a builder's scaffolding in miniature, and/or a bait that few self-respecting carp would take if they were starving. The possible,

Whiling away the hours in the bivvy making rigs is fine, but you can be a little too inventive – don't get rig-happy!

indeed, probable, problem arises though, when that natural fallow period comes to an end. For the end of that period could well coincide with that moment you try the scaffolding rig and/or the 'crap' bait, and the dumbest carp in the lake comes along and takes it!

The unwary, or the rig freaks, or the bait freaks, then begin shrieking, 'Hallelujah! I've done it again; I've come up with a rig/bait that has sorted the men from the boys!' And from that moment spend several more weeks blanking, or near blanking, when they could have been enjoying much better catches on the good old faithful rig and bait that worked consistently well before the natural fallow period came along.

So the message is, by all means try different rigs, baits and swims when you think it's necessary, but just do everything you can to ensure it *is* necessary. And for several sessions at least, ensure that one rod continues to fish your proven rig and bait.

How Many Rods?
Two rods is usually a minimum when carp fishing, with three as the standard for most dedicated carp anglers. Multiple rods are used to enhance our chances by offering different methods and different baits, or the same or different methods and baits in different areas. In essence, it enables us to make an each-way bet, rather than all or nothing on one likely winner.

For instance, the irregularities of the swim may mean that it would pay to have one bait on top of a plateau, another part way down the slope, and one at the bottom of the slope. Multiple rods give you the opportunity to target more than one

likely ambush point, and this particularly applies where you are fishing an area with islands and cut-throughs. Whatever the reason, it means you're going to have to work harder to make sure each rod is fished to its full potential. It is too easy to cast out those multiple rods and then sit back and let them get on with it, whereas if we fished just one rod we would be much more inclined to change things if we thought it necessary, perhaps bait the one swim with more care. It all comes down to focus, and there is no doubt that you can focus on one rod much better than you can focus on two or more. Don't allow two or more rods to become a substitute for water craft and thoughtful, intelligent angling.

Give some consideration to your fellow angler, too. Are you fishing a small water, or in a confined bay, and by fishing multiple rods are you going to intrude on the tight space that other anglers could occupy? Even if adjacent swims are empty, you should not prevent others who may turn up later from fishing them by having a profusion of lines snaking out from your spot on the bank. Of course such a situation could be covered by club or fishery rules, but a considerate angler shouldn't need a rule to tell him he's using multiple rods in a selfish manner. And bear in mind that fishing more than two rods requires two rod licences.

On a prolific 'runs' water you may find anyway that even two rods is one too many, and that you would catch more fish by focusing on the one rod and fishing it more effectively. Don't fall into the trap of thinking that fishing multiple rods *always* gives you an advantage; very often it is just the opposite.

9 PLAYING AND LANDING CARP AND CARP CARE

Be Prepared

One thing you must always be prepared for is the moment you land the fish, and that includes having an unhooking mat ready in a shaded spot with a container of lake water alongside it to wet the mat and keep the fish wet, especially in hot weather. Ready and waiting too should be unhooking forceps and Kryston Klin-Ik antiseptic to treat the hook penetration site and any other wounds the carp may have. Have your weigh bag and scales nearby in case the fish is a weight you want to check and record, and a camera should also be to hand if you intend photographing the fish. Don't leave these things packed away in the rucksack and then have to get them out and set them up while a fish lies in the landing net. Be prepared, have everything ready before you even cast in.

Be Organized

When you set up for carp fishing it is important to get your gear organized so that your rods are fishing at the best angle, are easy to get at, and with no overhead branches to restrict both casting and playing fish. Your landing net should be to hand no matter which rod you get a run on, and preferably with the frame and net sunk with the handle propped on a rod rest. All should be convenient and within easy reach. The unhooking mat should be within a few steps of the water, and with no obstructions that could trip you and cause you to drop and possibly injure the fish. Bait should be protected from the elements but placed within convenient reach, as should those small but essential tackle items such as baiting needles, hair stops, boilie dips and PVA. Ensure that none of your gear can get trodden on, be

This well prepared set-up of mat, net and forceps makes landing and unhooking carp a simple process.

blown away, is likely to fall into the lake, or might otherwise get wet or damaged or stolen.

Depending on the bank, you can use either bank sticks or a rod pod. Hard gravel can be almost impossible to get bank sticks into, and a pod is the best answer. Hammering bank sticks through gravel is always an option, but will scare most of the fish within a wide area – and not just your fish, but the fish that other anglers on the water are hoping to catch. Don't hammer anything in if you can possibly avoid it, and besides, the majority of carp anglers prefer a convenient rod pod. Whichever set-up you use, make sure it's stable, and that wind and water won't knock it over or cause it to move about and give false bites.

Your bite alarms need to be switched on with the volume set so that you can hear them clearly, but not so loud that everyone else on the lake is rushing to their rods thinking they've got a run. Setting different tones for each alarm will help you distinguish which rod has a run, although the alarm will light up anyway. At night, while you doze in the bivvie, a remote alarm is useful. It alerts you to a run and tells you which rod is 'live', ensuring that you're heading for the right rod even before you emerge from the bivvie. Make sure that the ground to the rod pod, or each rod on rod rests, is free of anything that could trip you, especially in the dark.

Playing Carp

One of the reasons, perhaps even the main reason, you've chosen to fish for carp, is their awesome fighting power. That blistering run, the rod hooped over to a heart-stopping curve, the reel's drag screaming in protest: it all adds up to some of the most exciting fishing you're ever likely to experience.

This type of rod pod is stable and versatile.

Graham keeps the rod low to apply side strain, steering a big carp from an island.

This is why it is important to know as much as possible about the swim you're fishing, and also the surrounding area where a determined fish could run to. If there are snaggy areas nearby, then you need to be prepared, both with the strength of your tackle and the action you're going to take to deal with the fish. If you don't have this information then you can bet the carp will, or at least have an instinct strong enough to direct them to the nearest snag or escape route. If there *are* snags within range you can also bet that the carp will head for them from the moment it feels the hook prick its lip. They have an uncanny ability to be able to home in on snags, and what they feel is the relative safety of them, with the same directional ability of a compass pointing north.

Fighting the Fish

Playing a big, hard-fighting fish should not be a battle of brute strength if you want maximum enjoyment from the contest; unless, of course, you are in a situation where there is no option but to use brute strength – for instance, when you have to bully a carp away from a snag. Bullying a fish is just one of the options you have at your disposal when playing them, but there are others, some subtle and some less so.

The first thing to remember is to use the rod, and if that sounds strange, it isn't, if you consider that many anglers allow the rod to point, or almost point, at the fish, thus negating most of the shock absorber effect the rod offers. Always keep the rod in a position so that it can bend, and the maximum effective bend is generated by keeping the rod at 45 degrees to the fish. This bend, or shock absorber effect, can be adjusted by reducing that angle, ie, by taking the tip of the rod towards the fish so that the bend in the tip section is reduced and more emphasis placed on bending the stronger butt half of the rod. Various degrees of pressure can be placed on the fish by changing this angle, while at the same time setting the drag of the reel to give line when a certain pressure on the line is reached.

A Possible Scenario

Let's take a look at a possible scenario and go over a few of the possibilities we need to be aware of.

The swim we've chosen is quite restricted on the bank as we're fishing between trees, making it impossible to move along the bank from that spot. Out in the water the swim is about 70 yards distant. No boats or baitboats are allowed on the water, so we've surveyed it and the surrounding area as best we can with a gripper lead and marker float, which is quite accurate, as we've learned with experience what silt, weed and gravel feel like when a lead is drawn over it, and the marker float is good for depth-checking to within a few inches. Some 30 yards to the right of the swim is a thick weedbed, so we know that if the fish runs that way, which is likely considering it is the only snaggy area within reasonable range, we'll have to bend the rod into it with the rod held parallel to the water – 'sidestrain', as it's known – which will have maximum effect in turning the fish to run in another, safer, direction.

The marker float revealed the various bars and troughs, most of them subtle, but there is a distinct one some 30 yards distant that reaches within 4ft (1m) of the surface, with the trough beyond it having a depth varying between 8 and 12ft (2.4 and 3.6m). So once we've played the fish with sidestrain to keep it out of the weedbed snag, we know that when we get to within about 20 yards of the shallow bar, we've got to swing the rod back to a vertical position and hold the rod high, because when the fish is boring along the bottom we have to ensure the line clears the bar to prevent sharp gravel or any other sharp object from cutting it should it rub along it.

When the fish is clear of the shallow bar we have to try to keep it over to the right side of the swim, because we know there are tree roots snaking into the water about 10 yards to the left, and although we should be able to bully the fish away from them at this stage of the fight, when the carp is tiring a little, it is better to avoid them in the first place. Very often the best way to do this is to actually pull the fish towards the side of the swim you don't want it to go to, thereby causing it to swim in the opposite direction. If we hadn't been restricted to a narrow area along the bank, due to the trees either side, we could have walked along whilst playing the fish, to an area more conducive to landing it safely. As it is, we're stuck with what we've got and have to make the best of it.

Knowing the swim and being well prepared for what may happen when you hook a fish is important, though, and being prepared for the worst that could happen will make everything a lot easier to deal with.

Don't get into the habit of backwinding, which is to release the anti-reverse mechanism of the reel and allow the handle to wind backwards as the carp runs, under control of course, but not to the same degree as the drag can control the release of line to a running fish. Some years ago, before reels and drag controls became more sophisticated and reliable, it was common practice to backwind. But not today; it's unnecessary, inadvisable and unsafe compared to playing fish off the drag.

When fishing at long range, unless you're using braid, 100 yards (90m) or more of mono is going to have a great deal of stretch and you're not going to have the same control over a fish as you have when it's closer in. The stretch in the line is going to have the benefit of offering more of a safety margin in the shock absorber effect it offers, but less in the control stakes when you want to steer the fish away from snags, or merely to bring it towards you. When a fish decides to run at you rather than away from you there could be a problem in retrieving line fast enough to keep up with the fish and keep a bend in the rod. If that bend should be lost and the line fall slack there is a danger of the hook falling out, especially if you're using a barbless hook. This is where a reel with a fast retrieve ratio – fewer turns of the handle to gain more line – is appreciated.

OPPOSITE ABOVE: With the carp in closer, Graham raises the rod to lift the carp off the bottom.

OPPOSITE BELOW: Don't be afraid to adjust the drag on your reel during the fight.

Graham with a lean, mean river common: 'The hardest fighting fish I've ever caught,' he said.

There are some circumstances in which you have to be prepared to walk backwards up the bank, as well as winding rapidly, in order to keep a bend in the rod. Never underestimate the speed at which a carp can run, both away from you and towards you, especially the long, lean, common carp that can muster an incredible burst of speed.

Many experienced anglers play carp as much as possible by keeping the rod low and parallel to the water, as described in the scenario earlier in this chapter. This applying of sidestrain applies much more control over a fish than does overhead pressure. Pressure to a carp's head from the side is bound to have a greater effect on steering it than pressure from above. The smart angler uses both side and overhead pressure according to the situation at hand, but it is as well to remember that continuous overhead pressure, which you see so many anglers restricting their fish-playing *modus operandi* to, is unnecessarily limiting yourself.

It is likely that you will have at least one other line in the water, often two, and this represents an additional hazard. If the bank side is clear of trees it may be possible to move to one side of

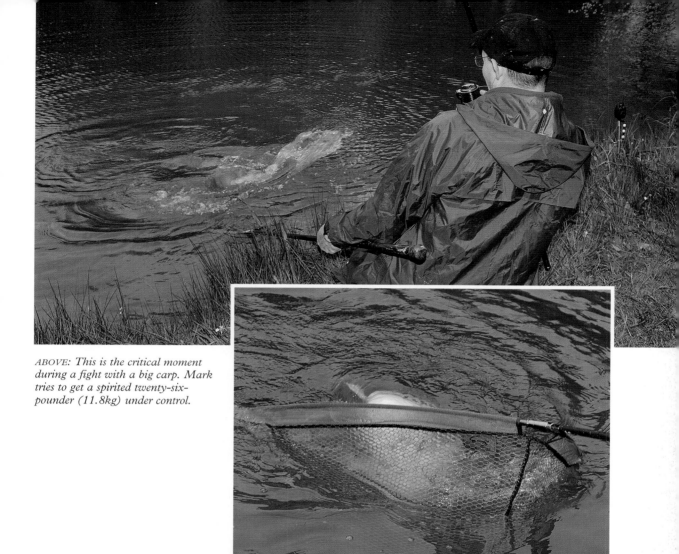

ABOVE: *This is the critical moment during a fight with a big carp. Mark tries to get a spirited twenty-six-pounder (11.8kg) under control.*

Don't lift until the carp is properly over the net.

the other rod and play the carp well away from the other line. The other alternative is to take the other rod, or rods, off the alarms or front rod rests and lower them into the water so that the tips are resting on the lake bed. This has the effect of ensuring that the line – both close to the rods as well as at the terminal tackle end – is as close to the lake bed as possible and hopefully clear of any hooked carp that are running over them. A clear head and a methodical approach are needed to keep a tight line on the fish as you use one hand to lower the other rod tips to the bottom. And should you be lucky (unlucky?!) enough to get a run on one of the other rods whilst you're already playing a carp,

then don't panic, make sure the line on the untended rod can run freely, shout to a neighbouring angler (if there is one) who can help, and continue to play the first hooked carp. And hope for the best!

Landing Carp

With a hooked carp tiring and under control we reach the next critical part of playing it: pulling it over the net. A hooked carp is the fishy equivalent of an adrenalin rush as it is, but it pays not to scare it any further by standing up at the water's edge to net it. Onlookers crowding

Grasp the frame and handle to lift the carp carefully from the water.

around are the last thing you want, so politely ask them to keep back or keep low and if a trusted angling friend is helping you land it, then make sure he keeps low, too. Ensure the net is sunk just below the surface and kept still, and only raised when the carp is lying within the net frame and not just passing over it and not under complete control. The worst thing you can do is stab at the fish, trying to net it like netting a butterfly that is on the wing; it doesn't work, and the

most likely outcome is a broken line or a fish that has slipped the hook.

This part of playing a carp is often the most frustrating. Carp, perhaps more than most other species, have an annoying habit of coming to life when under the rod tip. You will often find that it has been fairly easy and problem free to bring them in from where you hooked them, yet they can fight incredibly hard in the latter stages; it's almost as though sometimes they don't realize they're hooked, and allow themselves to be led to the margins like a dog on a lead, offering only a token resistance. Such placid behaviour is not uncommon when it isn't necessary to bully the fish, for it is certain that a fish fights according to the amount of pressure it is resisting, and the harder you pull at it, the harder it will pull back.

So remain calm and try to avoid piling on the pressure in increasingly frantic attempts to get the fish in the net. This is the point where you need your wits about you, being prepared for at least one more screaming run when the carp catches sight of the net. More fish are lost at this point than at any other time, either through breakage or a hook pull. Eventually though, the carp will come over the net and you can lift the frame so that it lies in the mesh. Now lay the rod down somewhere safe, where it can't be trodden on, ensure there is enough slack line, bearing in mind the fish is still hooked, grasp the net frame with both hands, lift the fish clear of the water, and carrying it carefully, lay it gently on the unhooking mat.

Playing and Landing Exceptionally Big Carp

If you've never caught a really big carp – say, one weighing more than 40lb (18kg), you could be forgiven for thinking that they are going to give you a much harder time when you play them. Generally this is not so, however, because when carp grow to such proportions they don't increase much in length, but pack the weight in the stomach and most often acquire a shape that doesn't lend itself to bursts of great speed, acceleration and stamina. However, to some extent they make up for this by using their sheer bulk in shorter, slower, but more powerful runs. Where a more elongated common or slim mirror of over 20lb (9kg) can muster a breathtaking and almost unstoppable run in the initial stages following hooking, a rotund mirror of twice the weight will run off at about half the speed and for half the distance – but it will be just as hard to turn due to that sheer bulk. So it's not that massive carp can fight harder, nor that they offer less of a fight, but that they fight differently, and in a way that you should be aware of.

Another thing to be aware of, when fishing from deep margins, is that you can have an extremely hard time landing a very big carp, even when it's been played out and is quite exhausted. The story of when Graham Marsden caught his biggest carp of 52½lb (23.8kg) well illustrates the problem:

I was fishing a French lake from a margin that was ten feet deep and I'd taken my bait out to about 180 yards with a baitboat. When I hooked the fish I knew almost immediately that it was one of the big ones in the lake, not because it ran off with any great speed, but because it behaved exactly like a big fat mirror carp usually does, by boring off in short runs and bumping the rod with hammer-like blows, just as though the rod tip was being whacked with a sandbag. It wasn't too difficult to control, for there were no nearby snags and the substantial stretch in the mono main line was providing its own shock-absorber effect, a little like using very heavy elastic on a pole.

It took me about five minutes to get the fish under control, and apart from the occasional short, thumping run, it was soon in the margins and, I thought, ready to net. Then the trouble started. Each time I got the fish to the surface and reached for the landing net the carp would wriggle its tail and sink down to the bottom. All it needed was its great bulk to get it there; no immense power was needed, and the fact that I had tennis elbow in my rod arm at the time only made things worse. It was dark and I was on my own, which also didn't help, for it was one time when I could have done with someone on the landing net so I could use two hands on the rod.

Eventually I managed to net it by standing on the landing-net handle, using two hands on the rod to bring the fish to the edge of the landing-net frame, and then quickly letting go of the rod with my left hand and grabbing the landing-net handle to push the net forwards and down just in time as the fish began its next trundle to the bottom.

The hook had fallen out in the landing net when I placed the fish on the unhooking mat and took my first look at it. I often think how close I must have been to losing my best-ever carp. I'd had a forty-six-pounder the day before, but this fish was just awesome and one of a very few 50lb carp being caught from anywhere at the time.

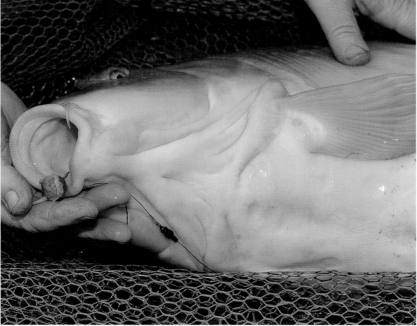

ABOVE: *Graham's 52lb 8oz (23.8kg) personal best carp that proved difficult to net in the deep marginal water.*

With the carp well hooked in the lower lip it is easy to remove the hook. This shot shows the sheer breadth of a big carp.

Carp Care

The water draining from the net should wet the mat, but if it doesn't, then give it a quick splash of water from the container you have ready. Ensure that the line and rig isn't tangled around the carp or its fins. Now cover the carp's eyes (some unhooking mats have a flap for this purpose, but if not, use a wet cloth), which will help to keep it quiet. If the hook isn't in a position to be grasped firmly with fingers and thumb, or if it's cold and your fingers are a little numb, use the forceps.

When gripping the hook, ensure that it grips on the bare wire of the hook, below the whipped line of the knotless knot so as not to damage it. Gently ease the hook out of the carp's mouth, steadying the fish with your other hand, and place the rig out of harm's way. If you intend

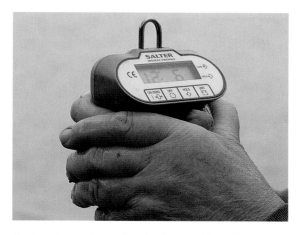

In the absence of a scales tripod, a good braced position makes steady weighing much easier.

'Hold it properly, Mark, and smile!'

weighing the carp then it will be easier if help is at hand so that one person keeps the carp still and the other wets the sling and zeroes the scales.

You may want to photograph it if it exceeds the weight at which you've decided a photograph is required. This may be 15lb (6.8kg) for some anglers, while for others it could be 20lb (9kg), 25lb (11kg) or even 30lb (13.6kg). If so it may be a good idea at this point to put the carp back in the water in the landing net whilst you get the camera organized. In good weather you can already have this set up on a bank stick or a tripod, but usually you just need to dig the camera out of the rucksack and ask a friend to do the honours with the shutter button (more about photographing fish in Chapter 6, page 92). Be as quick as you can preparing for a photograph, because every minute the fish recovers from exhaustion in the landing net the more it can muster the strength to wriggle and flap while you're trying to hold it for the picture.

Once the camera is primed and ready to shoot, either via self-photography or in the friend's hands, carry the carp back to the unhooking mat and kneel down with the carp on the mat just in front of your knees. Give it a splash of water, both for its own good and to give it a nice sheen for the shot. Never stand up whilst holding the carp and always keep it as low as possible when kneeling. That way, if the worst should happen and the carp wriggles or jumps out of your hands it won't have far to go before landing on that nice, soft unhooking mat.

Handle the carp firmly – don't dither! Turn it so that it lies on its belly and slip one hand under it where the pectoral fins are and your other hand under the wrist of the tail. Now lift the carp smoothly and look at the camera over the top of the fish. Finally – smile! Be proud of the fish you catch, be happy that you've caught it, and let that reflect in the picture. There are already too many miserable-looking carp anglers around who look as if they've had a bad dose of flu rather than caught a fish to admire and be happy about!

Returning the Fish

With the weighing and photography finished, treat the hook penetration site and any wounds and sores the fish may have with Klin-ik. Now slide the carp back into the weigh sling or, if the unhooking mat has carry handles, leave it on the mat. Lift the fish with the handles and carry it back to the water, to a spot that is at least as deep as the depth of the carp. Open one end of the mat or weigh sling and allow the mat or sling to flood with water and the carp to submerge, keeping one hand firmly clamped around the wrist of the tail and one hand under its belly. Most often the carp will realize it can swim off, and will do so with a resounding smack of its tail. If not, hold the carp in the water, making sure it stays upright, while it takes a few minutes to draw water through its gills and recover fully. You'll know when it's ready to go because its movements become more determined.

There is no greater feeling, having caught a big fish, than to see it power off, free again, and none the worse for the experience of being caught. Now swill off the unhooking mat, refill the water container, make sure everything is back in its right place, and get the bait back in for another one!

Safely and gently back into the lake.

10 LONG-RANGE METHODS

Anglers of all persuasions are notorious for fishing at the range they feel most comfortable at. In carp fishing, given the inherent ease with which you can cast long distances with powerful rods and large-spooled reels, that is usually somewhere between 50 and 100 yards (45 and 90m), and often more. Being able to cast accurately and feed the swim at long range is a useful weapon in any angler's armoury, as it gives you the ability to reach carp in far-off areas where they may feel safe. It is, however, rarely the only way to fish, so don't fall into the trap that many carp anglers do, and think that long-range fishing is the only option. It isn't, and fishing at much closer range can be much more effective provided you don't frighten the fish. Although any extra distance that you put between you and the fish is a decided advantage where disturbance is concerned, you can still keep quiet and out of sight at close range and have all the advantages that close-range fishing can offer.

It is a fact, though, that there are times when we have no option but to fish at extreme range: when the carp are obviously feeding a long way off, when there is nothing you can do about bank-side disturbance – such as non-angling dog walkers – and when you simply want to explore a distant area.

This 60-acre (24ha) pit has a low population of big carp to more than 50lb (23kg); fishing at long range may be essential to find these fish.

Problems

Yet in all forms of angling, whilst casting further can bring more fish into range, there are significant problems to overcome as you increase the casting distance beyond your comfort zone.

Accuracy is Fundamental

The first potential problem that comes to mind is one of accuracy. If you can cast accurately to within a yard at an easy 50 yards (45m), can you maintain the same accuracy at 80 yards (73m)? At 100 yards (90m) and beyond? If the answer is no, then you need to reconsider your tactics, or obtain some casting tuition, practise your casting and perhaps consider any tackle modifications that could help. But if you are several yards in error at 100 yards, and struggle to get much improvement even after a couple of attempts, then perhaps long-range fishing is not for you.

Be realistic about this, be honest with yourself; if you can't master long-range casting (and there are many carp anglers who never do, although they are unlikely to admit it!) it's not the end of the world, because there are plenty of carp waters that yield big fish at much closer ranges where you can be accurate enough to be deadly.

Remember too, that it isn't just casting a weight and bait, and possibly a PVA bag to extreme range that has to be considered. You need to be able to cast a big marker float to that distance, and be able to see it clearly enough to gauge depths and contours on the lake bed. You need to be able to cast a spod to that distance to feed the swim, or at least be able to catapult or use a throwing stick at long range to get bait to the swim. All those things have to be done accurately too, as well as casting the bait.

Accurate baiting is crucial to success.

Preparing to cast a marker float prior to baiting up with a spod; it is important to get the marker float exactly where you want it.

Realistic Casting Distances

The next problem is, that manufacturers' claims and practical fishing don't always match up when it comes to long-range fishing. They will claim that rods can cast 140 yards (128m) or more, yet such distances, whilst achievable in ideal and tournament casting conditions – no wind, and with a rig that consists of just a tournament lead and an impractically fine main line – all serve to deceive. Add in the difficulties found by the average angler who has neither the physique nor the technique to achieve these distances, and it becomes clear that we need to define much more realistic distances in practical angling terms.

With the right rod and reel, a baited rig attached, a shock leader and a main line that is suitable for practical carp fishing (12–15lb bs), and plenty of practice, 100 yards (90m) is about the sensible maximum fishing range for casting. It sounds modest against the hyped-up claims, but it is a realistic one, for it is a fact that there are not a few anglers who will never achieve 100 yards, and there are many more anglers who think they are achieving 100 yards but would be surprised to find that their estimation of that distance falls far short of it if it were to be accurately measured. On the other hand, there are some very capable distance casters that can add 30 or 40 yards (27 or 36m) or even more to this range; but with the problems of accuracy and feeding magnified, let's stick to the definition of 100 yards, and perhaps a little more, as the maximum practical casting range. If you find you can cast and feed accurately at more than 100 yards, consider it a bonus.

The Challenge of Feeding at Long Range

The next problem is how to feed at long range. Carp fishing includes a number of feeding methods: catapults, throwing sticks, spods, PVA stringers, PVA bags, sticks and Method feeders are the main ones. Each has its own skill, and you need to find which one suits you; thus where one angler can fire a catapult with great accuracy and over great distances, another could be hopeless. Even more so with a throwing stick, which can achieve greater distances even than a catapult, but there are lots of anglers who never master the knack involved in using one. Each of these has a maximum range. In the case of catapults and throwing sticks it is a long way short of 100 yards (90m) for most anglers, being more like around 75 yards (68m). You could conceivably cast a spod, PVA bags and stringers and a Method feeder to 100 yards.

Long-Range Line Considerations

There are other considerations, too. At extreme range line stretch is an important factor. Combine excessive line stretch with a big hook, and there is a possibility of poor hook holds when you lift the rod into a run. Some monos have more line stretch than others, so it pays to find a mono with minimum stretch when you know you will be casting to long distances. Better still, use a braided main line, which has negligible stretch – though only after you have made sure that your club rules allow for it, because a number of clubs and syndicates have now banned the use of braided main lines due to some fish becoming tethered with it.

In fact there is no need to worry about line stretch too much when carp fishing, because most of the runs from carp go off at a great rate, to the point where their speed, combined with you lifting the rod, is sufficient to counteract much of the stretch in most lines. However, it always pays to tackle up for the worst scenario rather than the best, and in this instance the worst scenario is a carp taking the bait at 100 yards or more and moving to one side or the other or, worse still, towards you, rather than away from you, in which case line stretch and a big hook can present a very real problem.

Playing Fish at Long Range

Ask yourself, if you hook a carp at extreme range, can you exert sufficient control over it to steer it away from snags or prevent it kiting behind an island? Again, line stretch at this distance is a factor to consider. Very often when fishing relatively close to snags and islands at long range, it is best to start walking backwards up the bank immediately you hook into the fish, keeping the rod well bent into it. This will give you those few vital extra seconds to clear the fish from the danger areas, rather than trying to repeatedly wind the rod to the fish and pump it away.

The need for a standard carp line of 12 to 15lb bs is more apparent now, rather than an ultra thin one of 8lb or so that aids the tournament caster. Indeed, when casting anywhere near snags or islands, the prime consideration is the fish, to land it safely and not leave it trailing any tackle, so that precludes using lighter lines to enhance distance. If you can't reach an area without a light main line where some form of nearby snag presents a danger, then the answer is simple – find somewhere else to fish.

It is useful to know what is between you and where you are fishing. Are there raised gravel bars underwater that can damage, even cut through, your line? Will you have to bring a hooked fish past other snags, such as weedbeds or sunken trees?

When casting a long distance on a water it is important to know whether your tactics will upset or annoy other anglers. Does it mean that other anglers are unable to fish their swims in a way that they would like to, because your line(s) cut across several swims? Or are you trying to fish where another angler is already fishing? Because the range achievable by carp anglers is significant – we have already agreed 100 yards (90m) is realistic – it is apparent that on many modestly sized waters, even ones measured in tens of acres, you need to understand where other anglers are already fishing, *or are likely to fish*.

These last words are emphasized because plenty of anglers turn up first on a lake, put out three rods at distance in different directions from the swim they've chosen, particularly from some kind of promontory, and then fail to appreciate that other anglers are upset because they are making four, five or six or more other swims unfishable. The argument that 'I was here first' cuts little ice, and you may quickly find yourself with few friends, as well as a ban. Some clubs and fishery owners have had to enforce rules around this simply because on small waters there isn't the room for such selfish behaviour. The philosophy is simple, really – be considerate to your fellow angler and such rules become unnecessary.

Effective Long-Range Fishing

Having determined realistic long-range fishing distances, we can focus on the practicalities. The first question to ask yourself is whether you need to fish at long distances on the waters that you are fishing. Are you doing it because everyone else on the lake is trying to outcast one another? Or does it bring certain features such as the margins of an island or an area of unfishable water within reach? If the latter is the reason, then it is all right. If, however, it is down to some macho casting contest, or just because you like the challenge of long-range fishing, then take a long, hard look at the water you are fishing. Where are the actual carp hot-spots? Can they be reached without casting long distances? Are there near margins where a quiet, simple approach may pay dividends? Are there other features in swims where the casting distance is much less? And is it easier to walk around to that far margin and fish quietly, rather than trying to cast to it and having to deal with all the inherent problems that extreme distance fishing involves?

Rods and Reels for Long Range

If the need for long-range fishing remains justified, then consider whether you are geared up to fish at long range. Do you have the rods and reels to fish at ranges of around 100 yards (90m) or more? You are probably looking at rods with a test curve of 3lb, although a well designed rod with a 2.75lb test curve may well do the job. As you step up the test curve the pleasure you will get from playing a fish is likely to diminish as the rod becomes more of a casting tool than the ideal compromise of a casting and playing tool. Not only does the pleasure you get from playing a fish with a stiff casting rod diminish, it also loses much of its safety factor, that shock absorber effect that helps you to deal with the sudden

lunges of a big fish desperately trying to escape the trip to the landing net.

Standard medium-size reels such as the 5000 or 6000 are unlikely to have enough line capacity to achieve long-range casting – their effective maximum is about 80 yards (73m). You need 10000 size reels, mini big-pit reels, or full-size big-pit reels. Then there is the consideration of what line to use, and whether to use a shock leader. For using standard leads to around 3oz (85g) it is possible to use a normal monofilament line of 12lb bs and achieve the distance without compromising too much on safety. The use of a shock leader introduces another knot into your set-up at the point where the leader is joined to the main line, although it is the only option once you start trying to punch out leads of 4 or 5oz (113 or 142g), or terminal rigs that also have to carry PVA bags and stringers of bait, or Method feeders.

Casting Technique and Accuracy

There is a world of difference between the casting ability of a top tournament caster and the average angler. It is tempting to think that it comes down to brute strength, but accurate long-range casting is nearly all technique. It's not so much putting the power into the cast, as getting the power out of the cast. The power that you put into the cast compresses the rod, which then releases the power. Like the best fly-fishing casters, the best carp-fishing casters make it look easy.

This proprietary spod mix has a good mixture of pellet sizes.

Professional angling coach Ian Gemson is one such angler. Using a standard 2¾lb TC carp rod he can punch a 5oz (142g) lead to around 165 yards (150m), although he will tell you that a baited hook on the line, and any other kind of attachment to feed the fish, considerably reduces that distance. Nevertheless, to watch Ian in action is a revelation; the power he can wind into the rod, and the subsequent bend in that rod, is quite frightening to someone who has never before seen a rod used to its full potential for a long-distance cast. And that is one of the main reasons most anglers will never be able to emulate Ian's casting prowess: utter and complete confidence in his tackle, to the point where he can completely clear any doubts about breakage from his mind and put all his effort into producing a flawless and powerful cast. Most of us, albeit subconsciously, hold back, we don't completely lose all our inhibitions about the rod or line breaking, and as a consequence the distance we can achieve, and maybe even the accuracy we can achieve, suffers.

Another point to remember is that the phenomenal distances that the top casters can reach are usually in ideal conditions. There are no bushes and trees behind them, no branches overhead, and no side or facing winds to compete with. In a completely open swim, with nothing to hamper any style of cast, it is possible to use certain styles that will achieve greater distances than the usual overhead cast that most anglers use.

A marker float in position; it's easily spotted, even at long range.

So, don't feel inadequate if you can't reach a swim that other anglers suggest they can. First and foremost we are at the waterside to catch fish, and not for a stiff rod-waving contest to see who can cast farther than anyone else. If you can't reach a specific area there is always another way, or another swim, that lies closer to your own bank.

Let's establish right from the start that casting *accuracy* is very important, a lot more important than casting *distance*. Where you have an alternative to casting distance by fishing closer, there is no alternative to casting accuracy. No matter what the distance is, accuracy is essential. There is no point in identifying a hot-spot if you can't hit it, and no point in feeding a hot-spot if you can't drop the hookbait in the same place – and not occasionally, but every time. If you can't consistently cast accurately, then work on it, practise until you can, and don't compromise. Casting accuracy is one of the most important skills you need to learn; it is a mandatory angling skill and one of the main elements that leads to consistently catching the fish you're targeting. So although there are specific casting techniques to give you maximum distance, they are not necessarily conducive to maximum accuracy; therefore this brief guide to long-distance casting will keep to the method that will result in both reasonable distance *and* accuracy.

Some anglers can cast accurately in spite of using an awkward style. The rod is held to one side, their hands are not placed on the butt in the best way to achieve accuracy, and they generally look as though the terminal tackle will end up in a tree rather than in the water. Some such anglers are often very good anglers, but you would do well not to copy their casting style. They can cast long and accurately in spite of their style, and *not* because of it.

It's always best, in the first instance, to adopt the basic stance and method that is usually recommended for accurate casting. Once you've learnt how to cast using that basic style, then you are in a much better position to make any personal refinements that you think may suit you better. Let's run through the basic casting procedure.

First of all, identify where you want the baited terminal tackle to land. If you haven't cast a marker float to your selected swim, then select a natural marker on the far bank – a particular tree or bush, maybe even an electric pylon, but something that doesn't move, and preferably something that will stand out on the skyline in poor light and especially when night fishing. That is your directional marker, and your distance marker if it happens to be a marker float, most certainly the preferred marker of most carp anglers.

Now stand parallel to the water with your feet about shoulder-width apart. Assuming you're right-handed (reverse the 'left/right' if not), you may be more comfortable with your left foot slightly forward of your right foot – try it and see. Hold the rod with your right hand grasping the rod around the reel seat and your left hand grasping the rod butt. Allow the casting weight to hang between 2½ and 3ft (75 and 90cm) from the rod tip. Bring the bale arm roller to the top, loop the line over your outstretched index finger, and then open the bale arm. Swing the weight behind you and feel it pulling at the rod tip. The further you allow the rod to drop back behind you (without the end tackle snagging the ground), the more

power you can put into the cast, because that way you are creating the longest arc, which in turn equals the weight moving faster, which in turn leads to longer casts.

Hold the rod above your head and make sure your right hand is pointing at your target. Now, imagine your rod is a spoke revolving around an axle that lies midpoint between your two hands and then, pushing with your right hand and pulling with your left hand, drive the rod around in a smooth arc, pushing your right hand towards the target and in a slight upwards direction, but releasing the line with your index finger at around the 45-degree point so that the weight flies upwards and outwards at the right trajectory. If necessary, feather the cast by dropping a finger to the spool and slowing down the line spill, and then brake it completely when the weight reaches the target.

Only practice will help from this point. Get a feel of the rod, feel the weight flexing the rod before the cast, and then feel the compression as it sweeps through the arc. The whole process is done smoothly; there is no snatching or hesitation.

The bend in a powerful 3¼lb test-curve rod when casting to long range.

Ian Gemson puts the rod under full compression.

Once you've mastered that, you can move on to more advanced techniques to gain extra distance; however, most carp anglers need only increase the speed of the cast to reach the long distances they require. You can do this by changing your stance so that one foot is more in front of the other, and then using your whole body to rock through a forward motion during the cast so that your bodyweight as well as arm power is put into the cast.

On a point of safety it is wise to use a finger stall, or a specially made glove, to protect your index finger from a deep cut from the line during the cast, especially when using braid. Don't take any chances.

Feeding at Long Range

Just because you can cast a rig a long way doesn't mean you can fish effectively at long range. Fishing a single bait on its own at long range is all very well, but most times, to do the job properly you need to be able to feed accurately so that your bait is surrounded by other carp-attracting feed samples: boilies, pellets, hemp, sweetcorn or other particles.

As we move beyond catapult range it is clear that there are a number of ways of successfully delivering feed at long range. Modern technology has provided some of the answers, especially in the case of dissolvable products such as PVA string, tape and bags. Different methods have their strong points according to the range, type of bait and distance involved.

Boats

For ultimate long-range fishing the use of a rowing boat with oars or an electric outboard is hard to beat, and ranges in excess of 200 yards (180m) are feasible. Rowing or motoring out your baited rig, lowering it in to lie untangled on the bottom and then feeding accurately over it and around it is the ultimate in bait and feed delivery in terms of accuracy and efficiency. Again, though, a word about safety: always wear a buoyancy aid, and never stand up in the boat unless it is tied to the

Precision baiting: Graham feeds the swim and positions the baits, while out of sight Mark controls the line from the bank.

INSET: This streamlined PVA bag will assist in achieving a long distance, but a PVA stick is a good alternative method.

Preparing to cast out a PVA stick, usually a better option for long range than a PVA bag.

bank. The whole boating process works better and is safer if you have a partner on the bank to look after the rods, ensuring that line peels off the reels smoothly, and to close the bale arms of the reels once the rig is lowered in. The biggest problem with a boat is that there are few waters where they are allowed; this is particularly understandable on smaller waters.

Baitboats

A remote-controlled baitboat performs almost as well as a rowing boat, and in fact in some instances it is better, because carp seem to have no fear of them, probably associating them with a goose or some other waterfowl. Baitboats are remotely controlled from the bank. They are usually double-sided so that a baited rig and an amount of free feed can be placed in each hopper.

The rods are placed on the rod pod or rod rests with the reels' bale arms open, and the boat is then taken out to the swim. The hoppers are opened and the baited rig and feed dropped very accurately to the bottom. The two hopper loads are usually deposited at least a few yards apart, if not in two entirely different swims.

Baitboats are deadly when used correctly. Apart from being able to deposit bait and feed beyond even exceptional casting range, they can deposit the goods in otherwise inaccessible spots, for example under bushes and trees, in areas where carp consider they are safe. And they do this without spooking the carp and with superb accuracy. Not only that, but the modern baitboat can be fitted with sonar to aid with depth and feature finding, and even fish finding, and some are now fitted with cameras that allow you, where the water is sufficiently clear, to actually take a look under the boat.

The disadvantage of baitboats is that they are banned on some waters, so be sure to establish the rules first.

PVA (Polyvinyl Alcohol)

PVA is the scientific abbreviation for polyvinyl acetate but that isn't the dissolving stuff that anglers use. Anglers use PVOH, a water-soluble synthetic polymer, which is polyvinyl alcohol. Calling polyvinyl alcohol 'PVA' was a mistake made by those who introduced 'PVA' (PVOH) to anglers in the first place, but time has made the name stick throughout the sport and the industry. Even now you will read in magazines and books that 'anglers use polyvinyl acetate' (PVA), but that is not correct.

It's probably too late now to change to the correct terminology, so for the sake of not causing confusion we'll go along with the rest of the angling world and continue to call polyvinyl alcohol 'PVA', even though the correct abbreviation is 'PVOH'.

In angling, PVA is used to create a small bag, or to string together, a portion of dry or oiled feed, which is then cast into the water attached to the terminal tackle, the bag or string then dissolving up to a minute later (depending on the type of bag used and the temperature of the water) and leaving the feed around your hookbait. Dry feed is used most of the time, but feed moistened with oil-based flavours can also be used. Be wary of rain, wet fingers and wet tackle, none of which are desirable when using PVA!

PVA String and Tape
PVA string was the first PVA product to be used by carp anglers and it is still a very useful tool to this day, although today PVA bags and PVA mesh tube are probably the most popular. Boilies are threaded on to the string or tape with a baiting needle, keeping them apart by a few millimetres so that the water can contact the string or tape. Most carpers prefer tape to string for that reason: the boilies are held tighter and are less inclined to move and close the gaps during the cast.

Constructing PVA stringers (with string or tape) is simple: just thread up to half a dozen boilies on to a stringer baiting needle, double over the tape or string, hook the loop formed over the needle, and then pull the boilies on to the material. This loop is then hung on to the baited hook for casting, and should withstand quite a hefty cast.

PVA Bags
PVA is available in many forms. The most commonly used is a continuous mesh roll that can be used to create various sized bags of boilies or pellets using a funnel and plunger system. Ready-made, solid bags are also available, which are more convenient to use and slightly less expensive but take a little longer to dissolve. The

advantage of a solid bag is that liquid (oil-based) flavours can be used. Many anglers simply hang the bag on to the hook, and at least with that method the feed is delivered tight around the hookbait. Others use PVA string or tape to fasten the bag to the terminal tackle, but some anglers screw a curtain ring into the lead and fasten the bag to that.

A small PVA bag can be filled with a mixture of pellets and crumbled boilies.

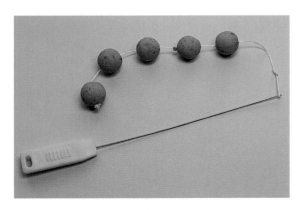

A stringer is a good way to get several boilies in close proximity to your hookbait. Leave a gap between each bait to help the string dissolve quickly.

By screwing a curtain ring into a lead you have an ideal way to attach PVA bags.

The size of the PVA bag you make can vary according to how much you want to feed at each cast, and the distance you want to cast (small bags cast further, but the cast is still limited to around 75–80 yards (68–73m). Where distance is a factor you can make more aerodynamic bags by moistening and turning over the corners. The feed used in PVA bags is usually pellets and boilies, with the boilies being whole, broken or crumbled, or a combination of the three.

PVA dissolves more slowly in cold water, so many manufacturers make bags from a thinner material for winter use. When fishing deeper water of 12ft (3.6m) or more, or when making particularly vigorous casts, the thicker bags are the ones to use. Flavoured PVA bags can also be purchased, but it is debatable as to whether they offer any advantage over unflavoured PVA bags that carry flavoured bait.

Making a PVA stick 1: Fill the stick with spod mix.

Dissolving or Pop-up Foam

Dissolving foam consists of nuggets of PVA that can be bought in various colours, but are mainly white. It originated as packing material, and you can still get hold of lots of this much more cheaply than that sold for fishing. However, check first that the packing material you use actually dissolves – not all of it does! Dissolving foam nuggets are useful because they are buoyant; thus when fishing over silt, for instance, impaling a nugget on the hook before casting allows the bait to fall gently on to the silt, rather than landing with a bump and risking becoming buried.

It has other uses, too; for example, folding a piece over the hair and shank of the hook ensures that a rig with a long hair doesn't tangle in flight. And many anglers use it to mask the hook point when fishing over gravel to ensure the hook doesn't get blunted as the tackle settles and is then tightened up to.

Making a PVA stick 2: Tie off the end of the stick.

Bait Sticks

The latest innovation of the PVA mesh bag is the bait stick. The method uses a very narrow mesh tube to form a long, compacted 'stick' of bait. They are made with a smaller diameter funnel and plunger than that used for PVA mesh bags, and are filled with a special stick mix that, when bagged tightly, explodes around the hookbait area when the mesh dissolves.

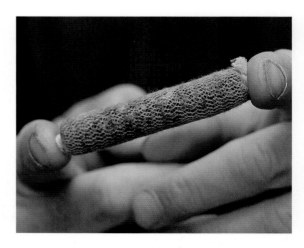

Making a PVA stick 3: The finished PVA stick.

With all the PVA methods you can make up bags that are ready to use either before you go fishing or while you fish. There is something quite therapeutic about sitting there waiting for a run whilst making up PVA stringers, bags or sticks. Just remember to store them somewhere, or in something, that will ensure they stay dry!

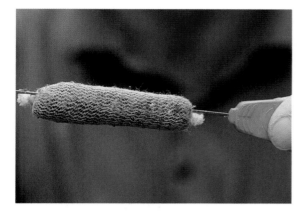

Making a PVA stick 4: With the lead unclipped, use a stringer needle to thread the stick on the hook link.

Making a PVA stick 5: Ready to cast with the hook masked with PVA foam.

Spodding

A spod, or a bait rocket as they're sometimes known, is a big, rocket-shaped swimfeeder used to propel bait to a distant swim. Unlike a normal swimfeeder the spod doesn't belong on any terminal tackle; it is a device in its own right that is used with a heavy rod and line strong enough to cope with the often heavy weights of bait associated with spodding.

Many carp anglers swear by spodding, and quite a few others swear at it, saying the noise and disturbance associated with spodding spooks the carp and destroys the chances of a run. Of course, like everything there is a middle ground, and the middle ground with spodding is to assess every water and swim you visit and decide which is best: the subtle approach where small and delicate food parcels are delivered little and often by PVA stringer or bag, or the much less subtle approach of the spod, where a generous amount of bait is delivered maybe once, or sometimes two or three times or more, in a twenty-four-hour session.

The bottom line is that you should get to know your waters and the carp in them, and make your judgement based on that. Never, in anything to do with fishing, become one of those anglers who only ever uses one method for everything: thus don't become a 'spod man' or a 'PVA bag man', or any other kind of 'man', but leave all the doors open, use your experience, and then decide which is the best method to use on that water at that time. Keep those blinkers off!

You need a powerful rod to spod, but not one that is just poker stiff: it still needs to be a rod that flexes and behaves like a rod. A length of 12–13ft (3.5–3.7m) and with a test curve of 4–5lb isn't too powerful if you're going to cast the largest size spods filled to their maximum realistic capacity (these can weigh as much as 10oz (280g)) to extreme distances. Most of the top rod manufacturers offer a specially made spod rod in their range. The reel, too, needs to be one with a large tapered spool, one of the biggest big pit-type reels. Don't skimp on the quality of the reel you use for spodding, because this reel will have to work hard casting and retrieving that big spod repeatedly when you're baiting heavily. A cheap reel will fall apart in no time, and that's just false economy.

The reel is best filled with braided line, because then you will have the lowest diameter line for a given strength. Braid of 30lb bs is about right, which will have about the same diameter as 6lb mono. For light spod work, up to about a 4oz (113g) load, you can get away without a shock leader, but for anything heavier you do need a shock leader to take the strain of casting that heavy load. Many manufacturers offer readymade shock leaders, or you can make your own from 50lb bs braid. The shock leader should be at least twice the length of your spod rod, so 24ft (7m) on a 12ft rod is the minimum.

Tying the leader to the main line requires a very carefully tied double grinner knot. This knot offers the least interference with casting in that it is not so bulky the knot catches too much in the rod rings, and it is very reliable. A handy tip, too, is to remember to position the knot at the back end of the spool each time you retrieve, which will keep it out of the way as the coils of line peel off before the knot is reached.

Most important is to wear a finger stall or some kind of protective glove to cover the finger that curls around the line before you release the line on the cast. Gardner Tackle offer a glove specifically for the job, otherwise you risk slicing your finger very badly; and anyway, a prolonged spodding session will leave your finger sore without some kind of protection.

Take your time lining up the spod with your marker float.

An alternative to using a leader with a knot is to use a special tapered line, like this one.

The end of a big cast – the follow-through.

There is a good variety of spods to choose from: some are just plain coned tubes with holes and a means of attaching them to the quick-release swivel at the end of the shock leader, while others have interchangeable sleeves suited to different types of bait. But they all work on the same principle, which is to deliver loose feed to the swim, turning over, via the buoyant nose cone, to tip the feed into the swim. Choose your spod according to casting distance.

When casting a heavy spod it is essential to protect your finger using a glove.

Don't overfill the spod.

Although there are dedicated spod mixes, you can spod any kind of free feed to the swim, but it pays to make sure you use the right kind of spod for each type of bait. With some loose bait, especially maggots, top off the load with a plug of groundbait to prevent spillage. And most important, don't overfill the spod: better to cast it a few more times than to suffer from 'spod spill', as it has become popularly known. Fill the spod to within about 1½in (4cm) of the top to ensure that it flies slightly nose down rather than nose up.

Casting a spod requires the same technique as casting any heavy weight, except for one thing: if you want to reduce the disturbance of the spod when it enters the surface you have to learn how to apply the brakes to the cast at the crucial point:

- The first thing you do is ascertain the distance to the marker – that is, cast your spod to the exact spot where you want it to tip the feed, pull off a few more coils of line, then trap the line under the line clip on the spool.
- The next time you cast you can put a little more effort into it, just as though you are trying to cast just beyond the marker, and then, as the spod is about to fly past the marker, hold the rod almost vertical and feel the weight of the spod pull on the rod tip.
- At the same moment, lower the rod but retain the tension so that the spod is eased into the water.

It sounds complicated, and indeed it does take some practice to perfect, but it is a technique well worth learning to keep spodding disturbance to a minimum. Besides, the distribution of bait from the spod is much more confined to the target area using this technique than it is when the spod is just allowed to crash into the surface.

Like any technique worth learning, spodding is something you can practise on a quiet water until you learn how different feed baits behave, which spod is best for certain baits, and to practise the spod-braking technique to minimize disturbance.

Whatever method we use to feed the swim, it is extremely important that we do it right, because feeding the swim is one of the most crucial aspects of angling, including carp angling: the type of feed, the amount, and the technique for delivering the feed are all very important.

11 SURFACE FISHING

One of the most exciting, if not *the* most exciting, ways to catch carp is with a surface bait, a buoyant bait that sits in the surface film of the water. Yes, carp not only take food from the lake bed, the bottom of a fishery, they take it from all levels, from the bottom to the surface, and in particular, directly from the surface itself. Curiously though, there are some waters where the carp never feed from the surface, or at least never feed there often enough to make surface fishing for them a worthwhile proposition.

No one seems to know why this is so, or at least no one has come up with a truly acceptable reason, for you can have two apparently identical waters, and in one the carp will feed very often at the surface, and in the other – a water that may lie in the same vicinity – they never do, not during the day, or at night, even when the conditions for surface feeding are ideal. So the first lesson is to make absolutely certain that the water from which you want to catch carp from the surface is one of those where they definitely feed off the top. A few visits to a water in the summer months with a bag of pet food biscuits to scatter on the surface will soon provide the answer.

So when are conditions right for carp to feed at the surface? Usually when the sun has warmed the upper layers of the water, not necessarily at the same time the sun is beaming down, for during a hot, sunny and bright day you often see carp basking at the surface and although you may tempt one to take a bait, it is not the best time to catch them. Later is better, either in the evening or in the early part of the dark hours. And any time during a dull, warm day, when the water temperature is steady or rising, and especially when a light breeze ripples the surface.

Greedy yet crafty.

Carp will occasionally surface feed in winter following a mild spell, but don't rely on it; just take along a surface-fishing outfit and a few baits in case the opportunity arises. When visiting waters where floater fishing is always a distinct possibility it is not a bad idea to have the gear and bait with you, for you would regret it if the fish were obviously surface feeding and you hadn't come prepared.

Floater fishing, as fishing for carp at the surface is most commonly known, makes no distinctions between big fish and small fish: all sizes of carp will take baits from the surface. But as is the case with bottom-feeding carp, it is the big fellows that take the most ingenuity to fool. One thing that is most enjoyable about floater fishing for carp – apart from the sheer excitement of it – is how much it can teach us about how carp feed, about how crafty they can be at times when they are suspicious of a bait.

Floater fishing is a very educational exercise, for both angler and fish. The difference, of course, is that you can actually see what they get up to when confronted with a morsel of food that they want, and may want badly, but are deeply suspicious of. There is nothing more frustrating than to see carp mopping up the free offerings of floating baits and totally ignoring the one with a hook in it. Almost as frustrating is seeing the carp 'testing' each of the floating baits to see how they behave, and then being able to pick out those that offer no threat. Carp are not clever, they have no intellect, but they have very sharp survival instincts that alert them to a possible danger. They don't recognize hooks and lines for what they are, but they do learn to recognize shapes they have previously associated with danger, and when food behaves differently to how it should behave when it floats unencumbered.

They do this by sucking and blowing at the floating food items, knocking them with their lips and tails, swirling close to them, all with one purpose in mind: to see which one behaves differently to all the rest, which one behaves as though it is attached to something. Very often they take the bait right into their mouth, only to blow it out when they feel the line brush against their lips. To see your hookbait disappear into a carp's mouth and then see it blown out again, or to strike at it even when you think it is well inside and you can't miss, can be both extremely frustrating and exhilarating at the same time. It is part of the magic of floater fishing.

Tackle For Surface Fishing

Rods

A lighter and more flexible rod than the general run of carp rods, one with more of an all-through action, is usually best for floater fishing. There are two reasons for this, the first being that most floater fishing is done at relatively short range, most often around the margins and up to about 40 yards (36m) distance. Long-range floater fishing is possible, but not usual, when the heavier carp rod can be used and the zig rig, of which more later (*see* page 155).

The second reason for using a lighter rod for floater fishing is to enable you to cast lighter terminal tackle and baits, especially when freeline fishing, which entails fishing nothing more than the bait on the line, and when this is as light as a pet food biscuit a lighter, more flexible rod becomes almost mandatory. With too stiff a rod you would be continually throwing the bait off

Waterfowl can be a pest to fish and fishermen.

A carp craftily blows at some bread to see how it behaves; he's seen it all before.

the hook, hair or bait band. A 12ft (3.6m) rod with a soft action and a test curve of around 2lb will be about right for most floater fishing, but don't be afraid to step up slightly for bigger fish or snaggy water, or down a little for smaller fish in snag-free water.

Reels

Apart from big-pit reels, your usual fixed spool, free spool-type reel will suffice, although a smaller one in the 4500, or even 4000 class is often used to marry with a light rod and fishing no more than about 20 yards (15m). Many anglers use a centre-pin reel, which is ideal for margin fishing, and great fun, too.

The Main Line

For most floater fishing applications you want a main line that floats easily and can be lifted off the water to 'mend' bows and strike with little effort; a braided line fits the requirement perfectly, and the Controller Floater Braid manufactured by Fox is ideal. A breaking strength of 15lb is about right, considering that braid has a much finer diameter than nylon monofilament. Mono can be used – in fact on some waters there is a ban on braided main lines so you are left with no choice – but be sure to choose a mono that is more inclined to float rather than sink; a good choice is Daiwa Sensor, although it's a good idea to carry some line floatant to enhance its buoyancy if the water is rippled and you're not casting

too often. Use about 10lb bs for mono, but 8lb is fine for smaller fish, and 12lb or heavier for bigger fish in snaggy waters.

Hooks

It isn't so critical when bottom fishing, but when surface fishing the balance between bait and hook size should be carefully considered. There are two issues: weight is one, in that the hook should not be so heavy it will sink the bait; and the other is that the hook should be as small as you can get away with, giving due consideration to bait size and consistency. Smaller hooks are lighter and less easily seen, but they should be big enough to offer sufficient hooking power – there is no point in using a hook that is too small for a bait that is so big it masks the point. This isn't so critical when using soft baits such as bread, because even a small hook will slice through wet bread and into the lip of the fish without any problem. Even when hair rigging, when the whole of the hook is exposed, it is still important to choose the right size hook according to the size and consistency of the bait. Curved hooks such as Korum Seamless are a good choice.

Hooklengths

This is probably the most important part of the terminal tackle for floater fishing, because you need something that floats, is of low diameter in relation to its strength, but cannot be easily seen by the fish. If visibility were the only consideration, then the best choice would be a fluorocarbon line, which is almost invisible in water. Unfortunately, fluoro lines are quite dense and sink more easily than other monos, and although we want the line for the first few inches from the hook to sit below the surface film, we don't want it to sink any more than that. Lines sitting *on* the surface film can be seen as dark lines across the surface, but lines sitting *in*, or just below the surface film are much less visible. We want a line that will sit on the water and then hang just below the surface film for about a foot before it reaches the bait.

The best line overall for the hooklength when floater fishing is a copolymer mono, which is pre-stretched and thinner for its strength, and has more of a tendency to float than other types of mono. Again, the choice of line strength is according to the size of fish you expect to catch and the type of water you expect to catch them from, with an inclination towards fishing lighter than you would for the same criterion when bottom fishing. For balance, choose a hook-length strength that is about the same, or 1lb lighter than the main line. Don't use a hooklength that is too short, especially when using a controller. A length of 5ft (1.5m) should be a minimum, but one as long as you can comfortably cast is better still.

Floats and Controllers

A controller is nothing more than a stumpy float that works upside down to a conventional float: the line comes from the top of the float rather than the bottom in order to assist in floating the hooklength. There is little to prevent you from using a conventional float for short-range fishing, especially when an unexpected floater fishing opportunity arises and you have no controllers with you. However, with a conventional float, which should be the shortest and stumpiest one you have with you, it has to be attached to the line with two float bands, one at the top and one at the bottom, and not waggler style, with just one band at the bottom. All you do is attach the float to the main line as described, attach your hooklength using the loop-to-loop method, and then pinch on a couple of shot for casting weight directly *above* the float. When cast in, the hooklength will trail from the top of the float. Instead of using split shot you can use a waggler with a built-in weight at its base, but still threading it the 'wrong' way round. However, a controller made for the job is really the best type of float to use.

Baits for Floater Fishing

The easy and flippant answer to what baits you can use for floater fishing for carp is 'anything

Two options for floater fishing: a 2lb test-curve carp rod with standard reel, and a 2½lb test-curve rod with a standard Baitrunner.

edible that floats!' It's a fact, get the carp in a good surface-feeding mood and they'll take anything. Edible? Some days they'll take lumps of unflavoured cork, leaves, debris, and on occasions, a discarded fag end! But the following are the standard, or popular ones.

Chum Mixer

Chum Mixer is a dog food mixer biscuit that most carp can't resist, and *the* most popular bait for floater fishing, of that there is no doubt. You can use them as they come out of the pack by banding or gluing them to the hook, or drilling them and mounting them on a hair rig. Or you can soak them for a few minutes and hook them direct by sliding them round the bend and on to the shank of the hook. Occasionally a pre-soaked mixer or other pet food biscuit tempts the more wary carp that are on the look-out for biscuits that have been in the water for a longer period. Off-the-hook methods are usually best for both presentation and hookability reasons, but not always, so it pays to try both when one or the other is failing.

Other Pet Food Biscuits

When the carp on your water have become wary of Chum Mixer, then you could fool them for a while by swapping to another type of pet food biscuit, one that has a different shape and maybe a different colour and flavour. All such biscuits are worth a try, and the odds are that you will find one that catches more fish than Chum on a pressured water – at least until they become wary of that one!

Pellets

Floating trout pellets and expander pellets about the same size as a Chum Mixer (about 11mm) are best. Again, they have to be banded on to the hook, drilled and hair-rigged, or glued.

Boilies

Floating (pop-up) boilies take many carp off the top, and are readily available in several different colours and flavours. The down side to this is that the carp have probably seen plenty of them and know what they're all about. However, they are always worth a try. These are best hair-rigged.

Breadcrust

Never ignore this as a carp floater bait. Many anglers do, thinking of it as 'old hat' and not worth a try, but this bait has been in the background for so long it is a new one to the latest generation of carp. Everybody uses pet food biscuits on the most popular waters, and the carp are so wary of them they will often suck in a crust of bread without even thinking about it.

A good selection of different-sized floating baits: Chum Mixers, floating trout pellets and specialist floating soft pellets.

Flavours

Most of the baits mentioned can be dipped or sprayed with a flavour of your choice to try to enhance them. Some anglers flavour both the hookbait and the free feed, but many times it's better to flavour just the hookbait to make it more attractive than the rest. There are some schools of thought, however, that subscribe to the view that both hookbait and free feed should be exactly the same in all respects so as not to alert the carp to the fact that the hookbait is 'different' – that is, carrying a hook. Of course, this comes down as much to how the hookbait behaves as to how it looks, smells and tastes. Invariably it depends on the water and how well educated the carp are that inhabit it. The simple answer is to try both on your waters and see which approach works best for you.

To use breadcrust, tear a big chunk (about the size of a matchbox) off an unsliced, very fresh loaf, slide a no. 2 hook through the crust side, turn it, and then slide it back through. Briefly dunked it will absorb enough water to give you enough weight to enable you to cast up to 20 yards (18m) or so (*see* photographs on page 56).

Lobworms
Air-injected lobworms can be great, but don't last long and are not always easy to come by. Also, injecting them can be a dangerous business. For some strange reason surface-fished lobs are either excellent or useless, and there doesn't seem to be much in between.

Speciality Baits
Some floater anglers make a special cake from highly nutritious ingredients. Such baits work well on some waters, but it is questionable whether this is due to the nutritious ingredients, or simply because the bait looks and/or smells and tastes differently.

Other Baits
It's a good idea to have a look round your local supermarket for any kind of appropriately sized food item, for humans or animals, which will float, or can be made to float with a slice of rig foam or cork. It may be unusual or quirky, but could be just what they're waiting for on your local carp water! Artificial baits, such as replicas of sweetcorn, tiger nuts, bread flake and boilies, all of which float, are well worth a try.

Methods for Floater Fishing

There are three recognized methods for floater fishing. These are:

- Freelining, which is nothing more than a hook and bait on the line.
- Using a float, or a special float known as a controller.
- Using a zig rig.

Freelining
If there are signs of carp right in the margins, then a freeline approach will often work best. Where it is feasible to do so, the deadliest method of all is to place the rod in two rests so that the tip just overhangs the margins, with the bait lowered gently on to the surface so that no line whatsoever touches the surface. Sit well back from the edge and hold the rod if you know there are carp patrolling the margins and soon likely to take the bait. Otherwise, sit even further back, behind some sort of cover, engage the free-spool on the reel, and make sure it's set so that line can be taken easily, for carp hooked this way can take off at a terrific rate and can, in a split second, pull the rod in.

Float Controller
Big carp that have been caught before are often well aware that controllers, or what they see as odd-shaped objects floating not too far from the food, represent danger, and they are crafty enough to keep away from baits in the vicinity of them. In the worst instances carp have been known to completely vacate an area where a controller has been cast or spotted.

On waters where the carp are not overly spooked by a controller they are useful for two reasons: the first thing they offer is casting weight, the larger ones enabling you to cast 70 yards (64m) or more – although it is as well to

Time to keep still and wait.

bear in mind that long distances make it more difficult to see the controller and to hook the carp. Of course, when using a heavy controller it provides a bolt-rig effect and the carp hook themselves, but not always: sometimes they need to be struck at as soon as the float disappears. When you need a controller for casting weight at shorter distances, try to use one that is not the usual bright orange but some other, more subtle colour, or even a bubble float type or a home-made one that looks like a piece of driftwood or similar.

The Zig Rig

This gives an entirely different presentation in that the line is coming from the bottom to the surface (or some point in between), rather than lying along the surface. When you know at what depth the carp are cruising, or if they're at, or close to the surface, you fix a lead on the line that will present the buoyant bait at the right depth. If you want to vary the depth, then choose a set-up that uses a running lead, because if the bait is buoyant enough, you can allow it to rise to the required depth before you stop it with a line clip or indicator. Use a mono or fluorocarbon hooklength that is less easily seen by the fish, but use a floating bait that *can* be easily seen, perhaps a fluoro yellow, red, orange, white or green pop-up boilie. If you want to cast a fixed line in deep water, coil the hooklength and tie it with PVA string.

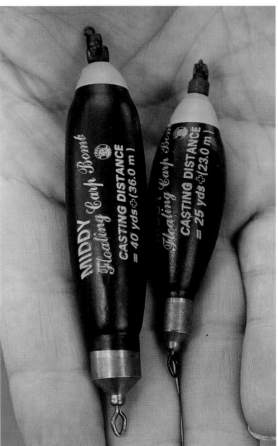

These shop-bought controllers have a range of up to 40yd (36.5m).

Two Approaches to Floater Fishing

There are two basic routes to successful floater fishing for carp. The first relies on stalking, along with excellent presentation of the hookbait. The second method has the emphasis on quite heavy and regular feeding, in that it strives to preoccupy a number of carp on surface baits to such a great extent it triggers the competitive instinct; they feel the need to vie with other carp, and due to this intense competition lose much of their natural caution. Let's take a close look at each approach.

The Stalking Approach

This method of catching carp with floaters can use loose feed, but does not rely upon it: it is not the basic principle of the method. You can use a little loose feed merely to test if there are any carp in the vicinity interested in feeding at the surface, to give the carp a taste of the bait you are offering, and to encourage them to look further for more of the same.

The watchwords for this type of floater fishing are stealth and caution, always remembering that you are stalking fish at or close to the surface, where you can easily see them, or signs of them. That means, of course, that they can see *you* more easily, too. So the first thing to consider is the clothing you wear, a consideration when stalking any fish, but particularly when stalking carp. In most cases, camouflage clothing for anglers is more of a fashion statement than a necessity, but when it comes to stalking surface-feeding carp, it becomes less a fashion statement and more a practicality.

It is essential to keep out of sight when stalking surface carp close in, for they will disappear like the early morning mist at sunrise if they spot you, or any movement that they regard as suspicious. So it's drab or camouflage clothing that will blend in with the surrounding trees and shrubbery, no bright and flashy rods and reels, and make all your movements considered and cautious. Being stealthy when fishing is always a good habit to get into anyhow, even when you know it is completely unnecessary. It's also a good idea to wear polarized glasses to cut out the surface glare and help you spot the carp.

Don't rush down to the nearest spot you can find, but take a few minutes to just look across the water. Although this is the stalking approach in that we go and look for carp, we may as well take a general look across the fishery first to see if we can see any signs of fish feeding at the surface. Look for swirls, bow waves and even little dimples that are often signs of carp just below the surface. In a rippled surface look for flat spots, those small patches of semi-calm water in the ripple.

Then take note of the wind direction, if any, and if there are any other signs of carp at the surface anywhere else, and head for the bank the wind is blowing into. This is the most likely place the carp will be, for the water is generally warmer

Using a controller led to the downfall of this carp.

on the leeward bank and, most important, to where the natural surface food has been blown. Remember, too, that on popular waters, any floating baits that departing anglers have thrown in will also be collecting along the leeward bank.

If you spot the carp feeding right along the margin, sipping their way along the edge of marginal weeds or right along the bank itself, then the first thing to do is fire in a few samples of your chosen hookbait and wait patiently until you see those rubbery lips sucking in and engulfing a few, growing in confidence with every mouthful. If the carp are feeding close enough to the bank, then set up a freeline rig, set the rod in two rests and lower the bait to the surface as described above, ensuring that the free spool facility is engaged. You can still use the freeline rig for carp feeding a few yards from the margins, especially if you use a bait with a little casting weight such as a pop-up boilie or crust, which can be dipped briefly to take in water and weight. Beyond about 5 yards a controller is needed. Always use the smallest, most unobtrusive controller you can get away with.

The Feeding Approach

Not all waters respond to the feeding approach; those that do are usually well stocked, not necessarily with small fish such as commercial fisheries, but with a good head of doubles upwards. On many occasions Graham has made catches of more than twenty double-figure carp to over 20lb (9kg) in one session, with a best catch of twenty-seven carp from 12lb to 27lb (5.5 to 12kg) using the feeding approach.

Correct feeding is the key, and this is where the carp angler can take a leaf from the match angler's book. Feeding should be regular, almost rhythmic, and relentless. Imagine there is a stream flowing across the surface of the water and you're going to feed that stream as you would a conventional stream. What you are going to do is create a feeding lane that the carp will find and follow, as they would follow the emissions from a swimfeeder. You need at least 4lb (2kg) of 5mm floating pellets, a few larger pellets and some Chum Mixer or similar pet food biscuits for hookbait, with some of them dyed a bright colour and some of them flavoured, too.

You need a day when a brisk but warm wind is blowing across the surface. Position yourself with your back to the wind and tackle up with a controller that you can cast 60 yards (54m) or more. Bait that up with a Chum Mixer biscuit, or similar, and preferably banded on for quick hookbait changing, and put the rod to one side. Now fire in a pouchful of pellets from your catapult to about 10 yards (9m). Allow the wind to carry that patch of pellets to about 20 yards (18m) before you fire in another pouchful, then another pouchful 20 yards later, and so on. The idea is to create an almost unbroken line, or lane, of pellets that expands towards the lee side of the water.

Once you've established that feeding lane, keep it topped up with pellets and a few hookbait samples, but now using the minimum you can get away with at this stage when the carp have yet to start feeding. Patience is needed; sooner or later a few carp will find the feed lane and begin picking off the pellets, their feeding activities will attract more carp, and the number of carp feeding will steadily grow and they will follow the feed lane just as river fish follow a feed lane in a river.

Don't be tempted to start fishing as soon as you see one or two carp picking off the pellets, but allow the numbers to grow to half a dozen fish or more. You need to see regular swirls and the top half of those rubbery lips hoovering up the pellets with wild abandon before introducing a hookbait. The idea is to get them sucking in pellets with a passion, to instil in them a competitive edge and complete confidence, to the point where they have abandoned their usual caution and are taking baits from the surface with the minimum restraint.

The moment of truth as a carp gets closer to the bait.

ABOVE: Koi carp often fall to surface baits.

LEFT: Graham with a cracking common carp.

Once you have achieved that, you can introduce a hookbait, and if you've done it well you'll find they'll take almost anything, and will be so absorbed with feeding they won't even notice when one of their number is hauled off to a landing net. What's one more splash or crash from a hooked fish when so many splashes and crashes are being made by hungry fish?

It is almost comical at times to see carp lined up along the far edge of the feed lane, top lips cutting through the surface like the dorsal fins of shark. Carp can be drawn along the feed lane from as much as 400 yards (360m) away and brought to within casting range. Just remember, patience is deadly, and pay most of your attention to feeding that feed lane; keep the feed going in, just enough to maintain the feeding frenzy and adjusting the amount (but rarely the frequency) as you observe how the carp are reacting.

So there you have it, the two basic approaches to floater fishing for carp, one relying on stealth and watercraft and the other depending on patience, to begin with anyway, and controlled and prolonged feeding. Both approaches will be viable on many waters, but on others one or the other will be most suitable. But that's where knowing your own waters comes into it. There are some things that can't be taught.

12 LONG SESSION CARPING IN THE UK AND ABROAD

If you stick to fishing fairly easy waters, those with a generous stock of mid-doubles to lower twenties, you'll probably never need to fish long sessions. A full day session or an overnighter is the most time you'll have to spend on a water to get the best out of it. Yet when it comes to the really big fish, the 'lumps', as carpers affectionately call them, you will need to consider fishing longer sessions of a full weekend or more.

The basic problem, if you can call it that, is that hard waters with relatively few really big fish are usually waters rich with natural food; after all, that's why the carp grew to such huge proportions – a full larder with few mouths to feed. That leads to the next difficulty, where angling is concerned, in that with so few carp for such rich pickings, they have no need to feed at every opportunity and there is every chance that over the course of a normal day or overnight session, the carp may not feed at all. So by extending the

fishing session there is a much better chance that you'll be there for at least one feeding spell, with the chances of this increasing with every consecutive day and night you spend at the water.

Long sessions bring other advantages. You have the opportunity to watch the water and make a note of the times when the carp do feed, or when they show and are possibly feeding even if you don't catch one. Over these long sessions you will notice patterns developing, particularly the likely feeding times. Such information can be invaluable, for it means that during your long sessions you can plan when to sleep and when to be especially alert, when to feed the swim and when to leave it undisturbed.

If you have a view of the whole lake you may be able to note where the carp are most likely to show at certain times of the day, which is useful to know when you have only a short session at your disposal and you can then choose the

The light is fading fast as Graham plays a big carp. Good organization is needed for landing carp at night.

If weather like this sets in you need to be well prepared to sit it out, and accept that it won't do your carp-catching prospects much good.

Camping Out

Apart from increasing your chances of catching big carp, long sessions mean you can enjoy another great hobby – camping! Camping out in a bivvy can be great fun, much better fun than conventional camping, because you have a distinct purpose to spending long periods in the countryside. The enjoyable camping aspect is one of the reasons so many carpers fish long sessions. And why not? Once the pitch has been set up and the baits are in, you can relax on your bedchair with a good book, or quietly listen to the radio while you watch the water, enjoy the wildlife, and generally chill out after what may have been a stressful week at work. The cream on the cake is that you have a good chance of catching a 'lump', and that all makes long session fishing a very pleasant thing to do. However, long sessions are only enjoyable if we have all the right kit to keep us well fed and watered, dry and comfortable, and set up to make the fishing experience a smooth and stress-free experience.

banker area to be fishing. You can tie in this information with the weather conditions, for over a number of long sessions you'll see which swims produce, or at least which swims have carp showing in them, when the wind is in a certain direction or the sun at a certain point.

Moreover, the longer you stay in a swim the better your chances of making a bait work for you. This is commonly known as 'establishing' a bait, which means introducing a good quality hookbait, usually boilies, for long enough for the carp to recognize that what you're using is nutritionally good for them and worth eating at every opportunity. Sometimes it takes several months to really establish a bait and often involves a period of prebaiting, but by fishing long sessions you have the opportunity to trickle your bait in at regular intervals, ensuring that whenever the carp visit your patch your bait will be waiting for them.

The key is that carp are creatures of habit with strong instincts. They learn which foods are poor and should be avoided, and which foods are good and should be sought out. They learn where the good foods are usually found, and even when they have eaten until they're full and wandered away, their instincts will eventually take them back to where they last fed on that desirable food. Fishing a long session gives you a great chance of being there when they return, with your bait waiting for them.

It goes without saying that you should have a good quality bivvy with plenty of room for all the extra items you need, to last for however long you intend to stay. Never assume that you will be able to keep some items outside the bivvy: the only things you can bank on keeping permanently outside are the rods, landing net and unhooking mat, plus any buckets of bait with firmly attached lids, and your large water container.

No matter what the weather forecast, the fact is that you can't rely on it totally and you have to go prepared for rain, however unlikely at the time, which means that many items are going to have to be kept under cover. And this is why many long-stay anglers, even when fishing alone, use a two-man bivvy, which is big enough to contain the angler and his bedchair, his stove, cooking equipment and supplies of food and drink, bait that isn't in secure and weatherproof containers, his rod holdall, rucksack and all his valuables.

As well as wild animals and birds there are thieves of the human kind too, even in some countryside areas, and you have to be vigilant. It's not been unknown for complete sets of rods, reels, bite alarms, indicators and rod pods to be stolen, and it can happen as quickly as it takes the thief to cut your lines, lift the whole lot and take to his heels. However, such occurrences are not common, and it takes only a few enquiries to find out if you're fishing a water that is prone to such activities. If it is, then you'll need to decide if long-stay angling is worth it on that particular fishery, or, as many anglers do, fish with a mate and make sure one of you is watching the rods while the other sleeps or is otherwise busy. Watch out for car thieves too, although on many of today's well run club and syndicate fisheries there are locked car parks and usually someone around to keep an eye on things.

Sometimes it isn't just the weather conditions from which you have to protect your gear, food and bait. You may be fishing an area that is rich with wildlife, especially foxes, which are becoming increasingly common in suburban areas, too; these animals are notorious for scavenging, and will nip off with bags of bait and food if you leave them unattended, especially at night. Rats can sometimes be prolific and a real pest, and you must be sure to keep all food and drink away from them, safe and secure in rat- and mouse-proof containers. And it's not enough to keep food and bait in plastic bags just because they're in the bivvy, because it's not unknown for rats to chew their way through a bivvy to get at food and bait while the angler sleeps. Be aware of the dangers of Weil's disease, a deadly 'flu-like disease

Outwit not Outwait

Although highly enjoyable, long-session carping can lull you into a catatonic state if you develop the wrong attitude towards it, as so many do. Too many carp anglers, often known as time bandits, think that this form of carping is only a matter of turning up with all the gear and staying for as long as possible. Some, who are on the dole or out of work for other reasons, spend several weeks at a time on a water. The problem is that they rely on putting the time in to catch the fish, rather than the effort. They settle into a swim, usually one of the banker swims on the water, regardless of conditions, and go through their usual ritual of baiting up, casting out their multiple rods and then settling back to wait for things to happen.

Eventually they will catch, there is no doubt about that, but this waiting for fish to fit into your fishing plan rather than you fitting into the fish's itinerary and fishing accordingly, cannot be described as good angling. However, if that's what the angler enjoys, then so be it, but he may not realize that he's missing out on the greater sense of satisfaction he could enjoy if he outwitted the fish, rather than 'outwaited' them.

After forty-eight hours of torrential rain and no runs, Graham's perseverance pays off with this thirty-five-pounder.

that is usually caught from rat's urine. Play safe and take an antibacterial hand wash and always use it before consuming food and drink. Never scatter unwanted food and bait around the bank where you're fishing, as this encourages vermin to home in on your pitch, just as you hope the carp will home in on your swim.

Personal safety should always be uppermost in your mind. Be wary of deep margins, especially in darkness, and never put a carp, no matter how big, before your own safety. So forget about swimming out to free snagged carp, or any other heroics, because *no carp is worth a human life!*

Supplies and Hygiene

Other considerations for the long-session angler are water and food supply. Food isn't so hard to deal with as we can manage with tins and packets of food that will last for months or longer. Water is another thing, though; you either need to be close enough to your vehicle that contains a very large container of water, close enough to some other supply of clean water, or have a friend at hand to watch your tackle while you drive to a nearby village to replenish water containers and buy fresh food and milk.

Personal hygiene is another consideration; soap (boiled lake water is fine for washing), towel, toothbrush and toothpaste. Last but not least are toilet rolls and a small spade to bury your ablutions, unless there are toilet facilities on the fishery, which is unlikely on many out-of-the-way big carp waters. And don't forget a small first aid kit: any minor cuts and grazes

should be treated immediately with an antiseptic cream and a dressing, especially where there are rats and the risk of Weil's disease.

Baiting Campaigns

You need to think carefully about your baiting strategy at any time, including during short, sharp sessions, but on a long-stay session of two or three days or more you have the opportunity to plan a baiting campaign based on your previous experience of the water in similar conditions, or based on someone else's experience who has been kind enough to supply you with information. This is not as daft as it may seem, because in spite of a few stories about carp anglers being ultra-secretive, most of them are willing to share information providing you are just as willing to swap information about your successes and failures on a water you're both fishing.

Very often, when fishing a short session, you have to make a decision about whether to feed heavily right from the start, or just a little. You have to take a chance, because you don't have the luxury of time to rectify a bad decision. With a long-stay session you do have the time to feed circumspectly at first, test the water so to speak, and then step up the feed in measures according to any carp activity you see, whether that is in the form of runs or merely observations across the water. If the carp are feeding steadily you may decide to feed, for example, half a dozen spods of spod mix every four hours for the first twenty-four hours, and then fire or stick in two dozen boilies over the top.

During the following twenty-four hours, if runs are coming steadily, you may decide to step up the feed, or to cut back on it if you think the carp are not feeding enough to take advantage of the amount you're putting in. But you can stick to the same plan of feeding every four hours. The other alternative, if you think the carp are spooking easily, is to feed the same amount but in eight-hour intervals.

These are the kind of things you have to make decisions about according to what's happening at the time, and you will get better at it as you gain experience. Long sessions will give you this experience a lot faster than several short sessions, because you have plenty of time to get to know a water, and to think and plan and experiment.

One of life's essentials – a supply of clean water.

Stay Put or Move?

One of the dilemmas that the long-stay carp angler faces is the ever-present question of 'am I in the right swim?' When you begin a long session, you naturally put a lot of thought into your choice of swim. You base that choice on a number of factors: previous form, the way the wind is blowing, which swims are available, visible signs that carp are present, the time of year, general conditions and your own general knowledge of the water. But what if, after two or three days of hard fishing, you have little to show for your efforts? Is it just you that isn't catching, or is it slow all round? Are the carp showing at the other end of the lake? Have the conditions changed since the start of your session? Perhaps it is now much colder, or the wind has changed direction. Given our ever-changing weather this is highly likely over a period of more than three days.

Whatever the reason, lack of action could well have you considering whether to stay put or move. It's not an easy decision, especially when it means dismantling a bivvy and all the other tackle and camping paraphernalia and carting it possibly several hundred yards to another area of the lake. In the circumstances, however, most carp anglers do just that once they're convinced that moving is the better of the two options.

ABOVE RIGHT: Baiting a swim is simple enough; doing it accurately with the right quantity and timing is the difficult part.

The popularity of this swim for long-stay carping is easy to see by the worn bank.

They've invested time and bait in trying to build the swim, and it is human nature to hang on to that investment in the hope that it will eventually pay off. Yet some highly successful carp anglers are constantly considering whether a move would be advantageous. They don't move every few hours – it takes too long to move anyway and they'd never reap the benefits of their baiting strategies – but when it looks as if prospects are better elsewhere on the lake, or even on a totally different lake, they are prepared to pick everything up and start again. That does seem a brave move, but their results suggest otherwise. It is very much a case of ensuring that you are moving for the right reasons, and not the wrong ones. You have to accept though, that you can't expect to get the question of whether you stay or whether you move right every time.

Fishing can be unpredictable at the best of times; you might move out of a swim after blanking for three days only to find someone else moves in and starts catching. There's not a lot you can do about it, but it is worth trying to understand why they started catching carp when you blanked. Did the conditions change? Or did they use a different approach and tactics? Perhaps it was just a simple case of it being time for the carp to move into that swim. It won't stop you making the same mistake again, but that is part of the mystery of fishing. If it was easy they'd call it catching!

Fishing Abroad

At some time in your carp-angling career you're going to consider going abroad for some of the special carp-angling action that is on offer. The warmer climate means carp grow to a much greater average size, and reach proportions unheard of in the UK. This doesn't mean our carp fishing is less enjoyable, just that every so often, once, sometimes twice a year, many of us are likely to head off across the continent to try to catch a carp that is beyond our reach in UK waters. Alternatively the attraction is to visit a foreign water where we can catch big carp in much greater numbers than we can here.

In mainland Europe and in North America there are many venues that offer outstanding carp fishing. The nearest country is France, and the carp angler is well catered for no matter what his carp-fishing aspirations. But France is not the only valid carp-fishing destination – Holland, Belgium, Spain, Romania, Canada and the USA are just some other countries that offer exciting prospects. The fishing is not always as easy as we are led to believe, but generally speaking it *is* easier than in the UK, providing we plan properly and go with the right attitude, and do not expect the carp to give themselves up.

Fishing abroad is more than just giant carp. There is a tremendous variety of waters abroad. Some are heavily stocked, small 'runs' waters

The world record carp of 91lb (41.3kg).

where you can expect to catch up to twenty carp in a day but with a modest average size – upper double figures perhaps. You will still have a good chance of catching twenty-pounders and perhaps even thirty-pounders, but little chance of the really big fish of 40lb (18kg) and more. This type of water is ideal if you're fairly new to carp fishing, having acquired a fair idea of how to go about it but lacking in experience. Catching plenty of decent-sized fish will certainly give you a chance to improve your fishing technique. Indeed, these middle-sized fish of around 17 to 25lb (7.7 to 11.3kg) often fight better than the real giants.

There are other waters overseas that are just the opposite: huge, almost inland seas, with a reasonable head of very big carp but extremely difficult to catch. These are the sort of waters that many very experienced carpers head for – and not just English anglers, either, but many top continental carp anglers target the monsters of these waters, too. The result is that the carp living in such vast waters are far from easy to catch. Specialist techniques and tackle are required, and the approach that works on your local 5-acre lake could be far from adequate. It's not just the size of the lakes that can be daunting; many have complex snags to contend with in the shape of submerged bushes and trees, or complex bars and ridges. You may need specialized gear as well as a boat or baitboat even to have a chance to exploit such a water.

Canadian carping takes on other dimensions, with a huge head of big common carp found in some Ontario rivers and lake systems such as Lake Ontario and the St Laurence Seaway. Locating carp is all the more vital when faced with a lake so big that it resembles the English Channel! Fortunately there is a wealth of information on the Internet, and guided holidays in Canada can make finding the carp much easier. Ontario isn't the only Canadian province that holds carp, and there are some good carp waters in the USA, too.

It all comes down to what you hope to achieve from your carp trip abroad. There is much to consider, not least how to get you, your friends, and a load of carp gear and bait to your destination. Driving isn't too bad if you live in south-east England and intend fishing in northern France or Belgium, but it becomes a logistical challenge if you live in Cumbria and intend fishing near Bordeaux. It could take you the best part of two days just to get there, and the same for the return journey. It all needs careful consideration, otherwise you will spend more time travelling than fishing, and be so tired when you get there that you'll struggle to make the best of the trip.

Once the problem of transport is resolved there is the question of what accommodation you require. On French waters this varies from simply being bivvied up, with no facilities and described in most travel brochures as 'drive and survive', to the 'middle-of-the-road' option where

A baitboat proved essential to catch this personal best 52lb (23.6kg) French carp from a big water.

Sauvellière, a French carp water, is a beautiful and peaceful spot to spend a week's carp fishing.

you live in a bivvy but the site has decent toilet and shower facilities. Some sites offer hot meals delivered to your bivvy door, or a dining area where you can be served with meals. Other fisheries have very well equipped chalets and log cabins around the water. There is a wealth of choice, and only your personal taste and available budget can decide which is best for you. The lake owner may provide bait supplies, which is useful if you need more bait or were unable to fit much into an already crammed vehicle.

Taking bait and food abroad presents its own problems, as both take up a lot of room, are heavy, and need to be kept fresh. The advantage of shelf-life boilies and pellets is that, provided you keep them cool in airtight containers, they keep very well – certainly for the duration of an angling trip. If you intend taking frozen baits, then you will need to use them up quickly or have a freezer on site. Much the same applies where food is concerned, so you can take tinned or long-life food and allow for getting fresh food and water locally.

Wherever you fish abroad, be aware of local regulations and the need for licences and permits. In France, restrictions apply on night fishing on many waters, and having all your gear confiscated *and* a hefty fine could ruin a holiday! Don't assume that you can just fish wherever takes your fancy, or disregard local regulations or the need for the correct licences. And much the same will apply in many other countries, too.

Angling Travel Agents

When planning a fishing trip abroad it is probably best to use an angling travel agent: they will ensure that licences and other regulations are covered, and will supply you with all the details you need to know regarding travel, the fishing you can expect, food and drink availability, local restaurant and entertainment places should you need a break from the fishing, and everything else that you may want to know. A number of well established companies offer a wide variety of angling holidays in many diverse locations, and if you are not sure about what you want, then these companies can help a great deal. They usually have websites that have detailed catch reports as well as the usual details of accommodation and location. This can give you a good idea of what to expect, the best time of year to go, and likely tactical and bait considerations.

Angling Lines (www.anglinglines.com) are one of the best angling travel agents catering for carp anglers. They can supply you with full colour brochures and a free DVD with still pictures and videos of all the lakes on their books, including the fish that have been caught from them. Their website has up-to-date information on all their lakes. They have a wealth of fisheries to offer you, with at least one that will suit your requirements exactly. They'll give you advice on baits, tactics and all the rest of the information you need to know, and more besides.

13 WINTER CARPING

At one time carp fishing was considered to be a summer season pursuit only, the species being much too difficult to catch once the serious frosts began in late autumn or early winter. But like the original myth from more than half a century ago, it being said that carp were too difficult to catch at any time, the too difficult in winter myth was laid to rest as each year a growing number of carp anglers proved otherwise.

Be warned though, in spite of all the winter carping success stories you can read in the angling papers each week, the reality is that winter carp fishing can still be very difficult most of the time. As in any season much depends on the conditions, but in winter the conditions take on an even greater importance and you need to keep your eye on them and fish for carp at the optimum times. Yes, of course you can still catch carp at times when the conditions suggest you shouldn't be able to, but unless you're one of those fanatical anglers who fish for carp no matter what the weather and just take it on the chin when you suffer blank after blank, and welcome the odd unexpected capture, you'd be far better carping when you consider you at least have a realistic chance.

Graham slips back a fine carp caught on a mild winter's day.

Understanding why fish, including carp, feed less as the temperatures plummet is a good starting point to working out a plan of action for carping in winter. Fish are cold-blooded creatures, which means that, unlike warm-blooded creatures such as humans, where the blood is a pretty constant temperature regardless of environmental influences, fish are hot when their environment is hot and cold when their environment is cold.

The significance of this is that whilst warm-blooded creatures have to continually eat to convert their food into energy in order to generate heat and maintain a constant body temperature, cold-blooded creatures need less food in cold conditions and are therefore less active. This is due to their muscle activity depending on chemical reactions that run fast when it's hot and slow when it's cold. The bottom line where angling is concerned is that when the water is cold the fish are cold, and the colder they are the less likely they are to need food.

However, there is a caveat; if the temperature remains cold, but steady, for some time, there is an increasing chance that the carp will feed at some point. Steady, settled conditions, are always preferable to any sudden changes one way or the other. With experience you will able to judge when the conditions are exactly right to go winter carp fishing, but always bear in mind that there is always a chance of catching a carp when you have a bait in the water and that there is no chance when your bait is in the freezer. Sometimes you just have to take a chance!

Keep warm

The first priority for the winter carp angler is *you*. If you don't keep warm and dry then you won't enjoy it, it's as simple as that. And carping by its very nature, especially in winter, is often a waiting game with prolonged periods of inactivity; just the formula that old Jack Frost needs to dig his way into your bones and make you feel that the last place you want to be is by a water with an icy wind trying to blow through you. Keep him locked firmly out though and there is no reason why you shouldn't feel good about being there and enjoying the anticipation of catching a good carp in adverse conditions.

Where keeping your body warm is concerned you need to think in layers. Start with a thermal long-sleeved top and long johns next to your skin; then your usual top and trousers; then a fleece and, to finish off, a wind- and waterproof, quilt or fleece-lined, breathable jacket and overtrousers. Thermal socks, gloves, thermal boots and, probably most important of all, a fleece or wool hat tops it off, preferably one with ear warmers. That little lot covers you for the worst days. For the milder days you can strip away any of the layers to suit whatever the weather is throwing at you.

You must be keen to stick it out in this kind of weather!

Bivvied up and snug – the best way to keep the cold out.

BELOW: Cold and bleak, this Hampshire gravel pit produces big carp in winter to those who make the effort: a far cry from a 'runs' water.

In spite of being well wrapped up there is still no greater comfort than being behind a wall of canvas in the shape of a shelter for a day session or a twin-skinned bivvy with a door that can shut out the wind and rain, snow and ice for overnighters. A shelter or bivvy will also give your gear and bait some protection and a place to make a hot drink and perhaps a hot meal. And that heat from the stove is always welcome on a really cold day or night providing you have adequate ventilation.

Most important too is to have a sizeable spare towel that you keep clean from bait and fish slime. Then, if you do get caught in a shower, through landing a fish say, when you've not had your waterproofs on and had to dash out of the bivvy, you can towel dry afterwards.

Choosing a winter water

The most difficult winter carping waters are those that receive very little attention in the winter months. It's become clear over the years that when carp anglers almost suddenly stop fishing a water in the late autumn the carp feed very little through winter and lie dormant for most of the time. On the other hand, if most of the anglers continue to fish through winter, and subsequently continue to introduce feed, albeit in reduced quantities, the carp maintain their interest in food and continue to feed. So the first requirement is to find a water that is popular with carp anglers in winter.

This doesn't mean that you have no chance of catching a carp from a water where only you and possibly one or two others are fishing through winter, just that your task is probably going to be considerably more difficult. All is proportionate of course with the stock level and size of fish in a particular water. Which means of course that if you choose a water with a generous stock of single and double-figure carp your chances of catching at least a few are very good no matter what time of year. Many winter carp anglers specifically choose waters with target fish that are smaller than they aim for in summer, just so they can still enjoy a satisfying number of runs through the coldest and hardest time of the year.

Locating the fish

Surprisingly it is most often the shallowest water in a lake where carp can be found in winter. This is particularly true on those bright sunny days, for carp love to bask in the sun and it's the shallowest water that gets warmed up first, even if only a little. Generally though, the same factors – temperature, wind direction, light and swim features – should be considered, although it has to be said that carp have a definite tendency to settle for a certain area of a lake in winter and stay fairly resident there for the whole of the season. Find that resident area and you won't often have to fish anywhere else, and being as most other carp anglers will also have discovered that area that's where most of the bait will be going in, which is a factor in itself that will keep carp feeding steadily through the winter. Don't make it hard for yourself in winter is the real key, and often the safest and best bet to locating winter carp is to visit the waters you have on your short list and note where other anglers are catching most often. There is no shame in following the herd, at least until you are experienced enough in winter carping to go your own way and perhaps at some time lead the herd.

Tackle and tactics

Just use whatever tackle you've used through the other seasons; there is no reason at all to change anything, for the winter will not bring anything different along to have any influence on the gear you fish with. There will be fewer opportunities for surface fishing, but even that can't be ruled out on the milder days.

Tactically, you have to be aware that there are going to be times when runs are at a premium through no other reason than the colder water temperatures, and that most times a change of tactics won't alter anything at all simply because the fish are not feeding. However, let's say, for instance, you're convinced that the usual bolt-rig-based method isn't converting bites into runs

OPPOSITE: Winter is nearly over, and in mild conditions this carp angler hopes his relatively heavy feeding regime with a spod will pay off.

due to the carp not being particularly hungry and not moving around much. What you can try in this case is a very sensitive running rig to try and detect those hesitant bites, and to sit over the rods ready to try to hit any slight movement of the indicator.

Baits

There is some contention about the best baits to use in the cold water of winter (when isn't there some contention about baits?!). We're often told that fishmeals are not easily digested by the carp in winter and oily baits are for summer use, etc. Most of the time though, if you have established a good bait in the warmer months there is no reason at all why you shouldn't continue to use that same bait through winter. There is nothing at all stopping you from fishing a non-fishmeal-based bait with less oil on one rod though, with perhaps the same flavour as your going bait, and see if the results suggest one is better than the other. The sensible thing though is not to get too hung up on the bait myths and theories, for it's a fact that there are no actual facts, only opinions and theories and the carp may not have heard about them.

Bait size and quantity is another question though, and whilst content and flavour may not require a change from summer to winter, smaller hookbaits may sometimes tempt more takes when the carp are not feeding with any gusto. Feed quantities most certainly need to be reduced from that usually used in the warmer months of the year, not all the time, but most of the time. There are some mild and settled winter days when we can pile it in almost as much as on a good summer day, but for most of the time we need to be very circumspect about how much we put in.

When you're not sure, or on very cold days when catching is not a good bet, it is wise to put in just a small PVA bag or stringer of freebies when you cast, and nothing more until you make another cast. Very often the best approach is to feed absolutely nothing and rely solely on your hookbait being found. For fishing the no-feed tactic, small, popped up, bright yellow boilies in pineapple flavour seem to work well on many waters in winter. Small bunches of maggots, fished with a blockend feeder rig, can be another good ploy when bites are at a premium, as can two or three grains of sweetcorn fished with a groundbait feeder with a few grains of corn mixed into the groundbait.

It is not a bad idea in summer, but in winter it's always a very good idea, to be really hesitant about introducing free feed. That slowed down metabolism of the carp may indeed quicken up from time to time and give us the impression they're up for a big feed. This may be true, but very often the feeding spell is short lived, a quick pigging out session and then complete shutdown for many hours, even days in the worst conditions. The only way to make the most of the carp's short lived troughing sessions in winter is to feed little and often; give them just enough to keep them interested but not enough so that they can afford to ignore your hookbait.

Winter carping can be a really enjoyable experience, particularly in this day of global warming where our winters tend to be wetter and warmer than ever. Many carp anglers prefer to fish in winter and catch carp very consistently through the period. Go about it the right way and who knows, it may become your season of preference.

14 FLOAT FISHING, STALKING AND SNAG FISHING

Modern carp fishing is mainly about legering techniques from a fixed position with multiple rods, and the only deviation from that is surface floater fishing with a single, probably mobile, rod. So what possible advantage could float fishing offer?

Its main advantage is an easy route to some interesting and different carp fishing that demands concentration but brings heightened anticipation for relatively short periods. Rather than all your carp-fishing sessions lasting at least a full day or night, a float-fishing session can be enjoyed when you have only a few hours to spare after work, providing you have a suitable water not far from home. Although the emphasis is usually on smaller carp up to 15lb (7kg) or so, there is no reason to assume that bigger carp can't be caught on the float. For the purpose of this chapter, however, let's assume that the main reason for deviating from the less active and more time-consuming demands of regular carp fishing with a bank of leger rods is to catch a few smaller carp with a more proactive method.

Accept its limitations, and float fishing can often provide fast and furious action when the carp are 'having it'. The carp you catch may fall short of those you usually target, yet with the right tackle they can be every bit as satisfying to catch. All it takes is a shift, mentally and physically, from the more usual 'trapping' method to float fishing's 'ambushing' stance. You don't need to sacrifice any of the time you spend trying to catch big carp, just put a little time to one side for the fun approach – two or three hours after work one day a week will do it, when the time available is just not enough to set up a 'trap' with two or three leger rods.

The first thing to do is choose a suitable water, one with a generous stock of carp, not necessarily a commercial water (although some have a good head of doubles these days), but a reasonably easy club water. Then you have to get into the right mindset for float fishing and the different approach it demands. As well as the fun you'll have catching carp on the float, there is an added bonus in that you'll learn a lot more about carp and their habits, which will prove invaluable in all aspects of your carp fishing.

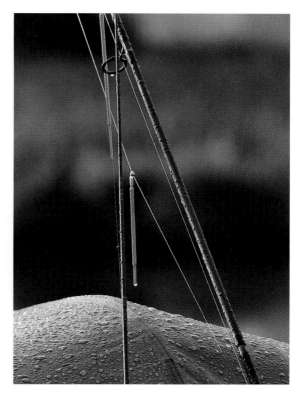

Float fishing is a neglected method for carp fishing, but worth trying for short evening sessions on the right sort of water. Having a rod set up for opportunist fishing like this is another option.

Float-Fishing Waters

Having found one or two waters that could provide you with a decent amount of action in a few short hours in the evening, you then need to find out what size the carp run to, and some idea of the best areas and swims. It is common to find carp right in the margins of this type of water, and this can include the margins of islands as well as the mainland bank. Even the most featureless of small waters will have its hot-spots. Often these 'hot' swims are created artificially through being the most popular and therefore the most heavily fed. Sometimes simple features such as lily beds or overhanging bushes will give the carp a sufficient sense of security to attract and hold them.

As with more serious carp fishing, spend time getting to know the water, speak to the bailiff and other anglers, and gather as much information as possible. Don't worry too much about the size of the biggest carp in the water, but instead get a good feel for the average fish. Remember that you are looking for hot-spots much nearer to the bank, up to about 15 yards (14m), than when you are regular carp fishing.

Tackle

Rods

When short-session float fishing we are tackling carp that will probably go to about 20lb (9kg) or so, but are more likely to be in the single figure to 12lb (5.5kg) bracket. To get the most fun from this type of fishing it's best that we step down the tackle from our usual legering gear to a light carp rod, possibly a rod designed for barbel fishing, or even a heavy float rod designed for tench fishing. A through-action rod, rather than a stiff tip action is better, as this will give you a better shock absorber factor when hooking fast-running carp, possibly under your rod tip. The length should be at least 12ft (3.6m) for float fishing, and a 13ft (3.9m) rod is even better, unless you expect to be fishing amongst trees and bushes or other confined areas, when a shorter rod will be more useful.

ABOVE: You can use the cover of branches and reeds to hide from the carp, provided you can still see the float.

This carp has given away its presence.

Mark relaxes whilst watching his float.

Reels

For float fishing, big pit reels and 10000 size reels are no good at all: you need something that is more at home on the lighter rod, and which you can comfortably handle better when casting a float and stalking fish. A 5000 size reel is much better, or even a 4000 size one if you've chosen a water where the fish are more likely to be big singles and not much bigger. And you don't need a reel with a free spool facility because the rod is unlikely to be left to fish for itself as it usually is when conventional carping.

If you really want to get into the fun side of things, with the emphasis even more on enjoying the playing of carp, then you could do worse than choose a centre-pin reel. A centre-pin will really test your fish-playing ability, but will reward you with some great fun. It is not the reel to use, though, for casting any further than about 15 yards (14m) or if you have a good chance of hooking a really big carp, although there are many carp-angling centre-pin experts such as Chris Ball who would argue with that.

Lines

Line strength should be a good marriage with the rod, so one of about 8lb to 10lb bs should do it, but don't be afraid to increase this if you've chosen a water where there is the distinct likelihood of hooking much bigger fish. A standard mono makes a good reel line. Braid is a bit too harsh at short range, and doesn't peel off the spool too easily when casting a float.

A robust centre-pin like this one is ideal for close-in carp fishing.

Hook links can be a thinner co-polymer line, but these do tend to be fragile compared to normal mono, so be extra careful when using one; in fact, don't use a co-polymer for this type of fishing unless the carp are being really cagey and you feel you have to. Perhaps better in some cases is to use a short length of fluorocarbon. In most cases you can tie the hook direct to the main line, fishing 'straight through' as it's known. Choose a line that is easy to manage when float fishing, because you'll have a relatively slack line compared to legering, and any tendency to being springy will give you a nightmare. You need a softer line such as Korum or Krystonite rather than a stiff, springy one.

Hooks

For the lighter outfits it is possible, indeed advantageous, to use smaller hooks than those used in conventional carping. However, it still comes back to balanced tackle and matching the hook size to the bait size. Fortunately there are many hook patterns in the smaller sizes that are very strong for their size, which means that you can use smaller hooks in some circumstances than would otherwise be the case, especially when hooking baits directly to the hook rather than using a hair rig. You can still tie your hooks on using the knotless knot, but trim off the hair. Use Korum Seamless hooks and you won't have a problem with the line bedding into the possible gap where the eye meets the shank on conventional hooks. The standard S3 Korum Seamless hooks are best for float fishing as they are the lightest in the range but plenty strong enough to deal with float-caught carp where there are no snags. Beware of the barbless hook rule on some waters, especially the commercials if you're targeting the bigger carp on any of those.

Floats

The usual float pattern for close-in stillwater float fishing in reasonably shallow water is a short waggler float. This type of float is attached bottom end only so that you can sink the line between float and rod end to prevent the wind or surface drift pulling it out of place. Lock these floats in place with silicon float stops. Split shot on heavier lines of 8lb-plus are prone to pinging off, and in trying to prevent this you are in danger of clamping the shot on too hard and damaging the line. When there is a strong drift on the water and you want some bulk shot down the line you can use olivettes, which are popular with pole anglers. You can use a swivel to attach your hook link, which will help to prevent line twist when retrieving some baits that tend to spin, and will also substitute as a dropper shot.

A range of wagglers taking from 3BB to 4AAA should cover most situations. Wagglers with insert (thinner) tips are more sensitive to bites, though most bites from carp are confident sailaways.

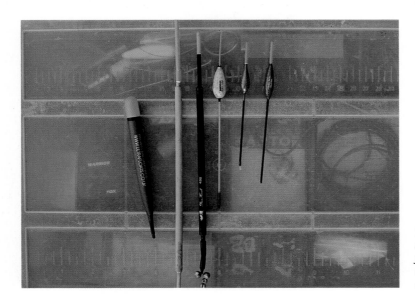

This simple selection of floats covers several carp float-fishing situations: from the left, a pellet waggler, two conventional peacock quill wagglers, and three robust pole floats.

Baits

Baits for float fishing need not be any different to those you use when legering, except that when casting to bubblers along the margins, maggots and worms can be the best bet. Beware, though, because bubbling carp can be very hard to catch. Even though they are obviously feeding, they are usually feeding on natural food creatures to the exclusion of everything else. They become totally preoccupied with bloodworm or some other small natural that is unsuitable for mounting on a hook that is big enough to land carp. The closest baits to the natural that we mount on a fairly substantial hook are maggots and worms, with a bunch of small redworms being the favourite. Even then, much of the time, when you do get a bite, it's due to the carp hoovering up your bait along with whatever it's focused on eating.

Yet another way is to bait up heavily with a small particle such as hemp, along with a larger particle such as sweetcorn, and try to tempt the carp away from their preoccupation, or to swap being preoccupied on one bait to being preoccupied with another, but one more suitable as a hookbait. Get them rooting for the hemp and corn, and fish corn on the hair. A good ploy is to fish one or two real grains of corn and one grain of imitation corn; this will make the bait almost buoyant – it can be critically balanced with heavy metal putty – and consequently much easier for a carp to suck in as it hoovers up the particles.

Tackling Up Tactics

Because you are likely to be fishing for short sessions and very close in, it is important to ensure that when you approach your chosen swim you avoid scaring the carp. That means keeping low, treading gently, tackling up at some distance back from the margins, and getting into position with the minimum of fuss. Use a roving chair to keep low down, and get yourself organized before you start fishing so that you don't have to keep standing up every time you want to re-cast or to land a fish. Have your landing net within easy reach on one side, with bait and tackle bits equally close. Then you can concentrate on fishing a swim with the least possible movement.

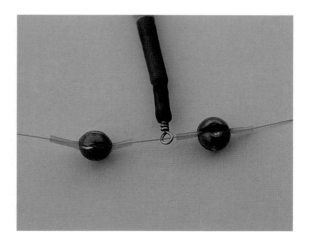

ABOVE RIGHT: Use thin silicone tube to protect the main line when pinching shot on to it.

The carp are feeding hungrily alongside the lilies.

Choose your swim with care, and study the possibilities should you hook a fish. Think about whether the carp are likely to run into weed or snags. Consider, too, whether it's the sort of swim that will come to life at a certain time of day. This is true on many popular day-ticket waters where the average angler starts fishing at about eight or nine o'clock in the morning, and packs up in mid- or late afternoon to beat the evening traffic. Typically, these anglers discard their unused bait in the margins when they pack up, and the carp soon learn to take advantage of this free feast. On many waters, particularly where matches are fished and end at specific times, the carp switch on like magic about an hour after the cry of 'all out'! Often it is the case that during the middle part of the day the anglers only catch the carp at range, yet in the early evening the carp move in to touching distance of the bank. Thus by starting much later in the day and fishing into the evening you can catch far more carp very close in than the day anglers manage all day. A further bonus is that it is usually the bigger carp that take advantage of the evening feast in the margins.

Mark caught this 19lb (8.5kg) common whilst float fishing.

Feeding

Good feeding can make or break your float-fishing session. How much to feed and how often are the main keys to success. The advantage you have at short range is that you can loose feed, which means you can do so frequently and regularly without any disturbance. It pays to take full advantage of this, as it will be one of the few chances you get to feed so often without disturbance and the inherent danger of spooking the carp.

One feeding tactic for float fishing is to put enough hemp, small pellet, maggots or casters in to get a small bed of bait on the bottom. At close range this is easy to achieve, and you should aim to get the feeding area to be about a square yard. Then, feed sparingly but regularly over the top of it. This way you won't scare the carp by feeding great handfuls of bait on their heads yet they will find enough to hold their attention. There will come a time when you will need to top up the swim with a more substantial amount of bait, and the best time to do this is immediately after landing a carp when the swim is already disturbed. The remainder of a group of carp usually temporarily vacate the swim when you play a carp but quickly return when it's quiet again. On many swims you will know when you've got the feeding right by the discoloured water, the bubbling and the frequent bites.

Float-Fishing Tactics

When float fishing the rig should be kept simple, nothing more fancy than two shot to lock the float and a single shot to lie on the bottom. This bottom shot will vary in size according to the conditions on the day: a calm water with no undertow can be fished with a single BB, whereas a choppy water may require as much as a single SSG. It is true that you could get away with a no. 4 or even smaller bottom shot on a calm day, at least as far as holding bottom is concerned, but when you're fishing for big, powerful fish such as carp, just the mere wave of a big paddle of a tail from a foot away will disturb such a small shot and give you false bites.

When fishing for big carp of double figures and bigger you have to fish over-depth in order to avoid line bites, not just from the carp actually touching the line, but to avoid the considerable water disturbance around the hookbait when the carp is circling around and rooting in the area. The aim is to have at least 1ft (30cm) of line laying on the bottom, and on occasion 2ft (60cm) is not too much when there is a lot of carp activity around the hookbait. Providing the line is kept fairly straight to the float, and reasonably tight from the float to the rod tip, bites will be seen as soon as the fish moves the bait even slightly. What you have to do is cast well beyond the swim, something like 3–4 yards (2.7–3.6m), and brake the cast just before it lands on the surface to make sure the line lands straight. Then you draw back to the position where you want the bait to sink, place the rod in two rests close to hand, and tighten to the float to stand it up. It's an exaggerated laying-on float method which is necessary to avoid false bites. Match anglers deal with the problem a different way, possibly a better way where smaller carp are concerned; when they float fish the margins they present the hookbait 2 feet away from the baited area.

Building the Swim

It takes time for the carp to settle after the disturbance of tackling up and feeding, so be patient, quiet, and don't forget to keep feeding on a regular basis. You may get other species such as roach at first. Don't worry; the feeding activity will help attract the carp to your swim. It may be an hour or two before the action starts, but once the carp are in the swim they soon push out the lesser species.

Conventional float fishing is usually accomplished sitting bolt upright on the edge of the bank, but as you are trying to catch big fish very close in, it will pay to have a much lower profile by using a low roving chair and sitting much further back.

Playing Carp on a Short Line

Keep in mind that hooking carp at close quarters means that you are fishing a short line and don't have the benefit of considerable line stretch when fishing at range, unless of course you're fishing a braided main line. So be prepared for that headlong dash for distant parts. Ensure that the reel's drag is set to give line, but grudgingly;

make the fish work hard for its freedom and as a consequence, tire it as quickly as possible. If there are snags nearby then you can be sure it will head for those, which means you can't afford to have the drag set too lightly and also that you'll need to step up the strength of the tackle somewhat.

Stalking

There is another way to develop the 'travelling light' approach to carp fishing, and that is by stalking them, ambushing rather than setting traps. You'll need a water that allows you to sneak up on them; it is likely that small, snaggy waters with lots of bankside features such as reeds, rushes, bushes, weedbeds and lily beds are the sort of water that provide the best opportunities for this style of fishing. Some bigger waters, notably estate lakes and the older established gravel pits, can also provide ideal stalking country, especially if there is a multitude of back bays and fallen trees. Before you embark on this type of fishing, spend some time finding a suitable water. The ideal water is not too crowded and has a sufficient head of sizeable carp that are not too difficult to catch.

Stalking Gear and Snaggy Swims

The essential aspect of stalking is to travel very light; the ideal is a small holdall with a tackle box that holds all your odds and ends, a selection of baits, and perhaps a set of scales, a weigh sling and a camera if you think you may catch that special fish. Other than that you need a rod, reel and a landing net. An unhooking mat will double up as something to sit on. Geared up this way you can easily and quietly walk round the water and feed a few likely swims and then travel from

ABOVE LEFT: A float-caught carp comes to the net.

Mark sneaks up on a classic ambush swim.

swim to swim, trying a hookbait in each one, beginning with the first swim you baited.

Your choice of rod and reel depends on the type of swim you'll be fishing. In open, snag-free water where the carp don't grow too big you can afford to take a lighter outfit, and then gradually get heavier as the fish get bigger and the swims more snaggy.

Snag Fishing

By its very nature stalking usually involves fishing areas where there are snags in the shape of fallen trees, branches and prolific weedbeds. It's in such areas that the carp take sanctuary, a place where they feel safe from natural predators and the ultimate predator, the angler. Very often you need to use stepped-up gear: heavier rods, and lines a few pounds heavier than normal. In those areas where you need to go commando style and work your way into tight, very overgrown spots, there are special short stalking rods available that have a standard test curve of around 3lb but are only 8 or 9ft (2.4 or 2.7m) long, thus offering more power. Generally, rods with an all-through action are best for short-range stalking and snag fishing, rods with which you can pile on the pressure but in such a way the pressure isn't too harsh. As a way of explanation, think about snapping a length of line you're holding between gloved hands. By applying a strong and sudden pull, the line breaks much more easily than if you were to try to break it by applying a steady pull.

The first thing to remember is that as well as having to balance the tackle you use, you also need some well-balanced reasons for snag fishing in the first place. Of course, the simple answer is that you want to snag-fish because the fish are there, they have succumbed to the never-ending angling pressure found in open water, and at least most of the time, hide away in a safe haven, which is usually a labyrinth of tree roots or branches or thick weed. So safe that they tend to feed in, or very close to, that area with a lot more confidence than they do elsewhere. It's hard for any angler to resist having a go for them, but if you think for one second that the odds are very much stacked against landing them from such places, then don't bother. The welfare of the carp should always come first. Otherwise, make sure that you, and your gear, are up to the job.

To extract fish from snags, or to prevent them from getting into nearby snags, you have to use strong tackle. That's common sense, but it needs mentioning because there are anglers who think they can snag-fish effectively with too light gear through fancy rod work: 'Just pull them towards the snag and they'll swim away from it.' Well, that may work for average carp on match gear, but these are lumps we're talking about catching, and strong rods, heavy lines and tough hooks are essential, and there should be no compromise.

Balanced Tackle

The rule of thumb is simple: a) the line should break before the rod locks solid, and b) the rod should be able to bend to at least its full test curve (the tip at right angles to the butt) before the line breaks. If 'a' doesn't apply, then either the rod isn't strong enough, or the line is too strong. If 'b' doesn't apply, then either the rod is too strong or the line is too weak. Put more simply, the rod and line should be matched so that the rod can bend to its full potential, but not to the point where it locks solid.

That's the first thing to get right, and the second is to make sure you use a heavy gauge hook. There is no point marrying the rod and line together and then using a hook that will either bend or break under the pressure you need to apply. Furthermore, fine wire hooks have no place in snag fishing because of the potential damage they can cause to the fish's mouth due to the cheese-cutter effect. Use a very strong, thick wire hook, and that won't happen.

'Playing' Technique

Too many anglers don't use their gear to its full potential. It's not uncommon to see anglers pussy-footing around with 3lb TC rods and 15lb line when the fish is heading for a snag or a neighbour's swim, when all they need to do is bend the rod properly into the fish and either stop it or turn it. At some time or other you must have been snagged and had to pull to free it or to break it. And when you've been using 10lb or heavier line there must have been times when you've really struggled to break the line. You've pointed the rod at the snag and pulled. You've actually

felt the line stretch and couldn't believe it when it didn't break until you pulled far more than you would have thought possible. Breaking well tied 15lb or heavier line takes some doing, and often involves taking several backward steps in order to do it, especially when using stretchy mono.

Some consider snag fishing as 'pulling the carp's head off', so how can something so raw and brutal be described as a 'technique'? But this is where most would-be snag fishers make their mistake, because they think it is just a crude heaving exercise between man and fish, with more luck than judgement ruling the day. Of course, a lot of heaving is involved, and like many aspects of fishing, there is some luck involved, too.

However, the first thing you have to get right is your attitude of mind. When you hook a big fish in, or close to, a snag, you need it to be firmly planted in your mind that you are going to bend that rod to a point where it may never have

LEFT: *Mark piles on the pressure in a tight corner; don't be afraid to put a serious bend in the rod.*

BELOW: *This quiet corner is a channel between an island and the main bank and is ideal for stalking, but you'll need your wits about you to play and land carp in such a tight spot.*

Graham keeps well back from the bank where there are several big carp just a couple of feet from the margin.

been before. You are going to feel the handle bend and creak under your fingers, and you are going to see that rod take on a curve that you never thought was possible. Keep those times when you've had to pull for a break firmly in mind. Remember them well the next time you go snag fishing, for they will help you to break through that psychological barrier that sets apart good snag fishers from the rest.

The second important point to remember is that you do not sit back from the rod as is the norm: you sit right by the rod with the butt within easy reach and the reel's drag tightened down. There should be no hesitation whatsoever in lifting the rod when you get a bite. When snag fishing, what you have to realize is that the bite and the run are one and the same thing. As the fish picks up the bait it immediately realizes that it has made a mistake, and heads off for the thick of the snag. You should be ready to counter that 'bite-n-run' before it can develop into a fast run and therefore a greater force to counter. The idea is to pile the pressure on the fish before it can develop the speed and acceleration it needs to dig in. The mathematical formula says speed is equal to the distance moved/time taken, and force is equal to mass multiplied by acceleration. Where snag fishing is concerned, that equates to not allowing the fish any time to move any

distance in order to develop sufficient speed to build enough force to beat you!

What happens is this: you get an indication, so you lift the rod and bend it – really bend it. The fish will try to bend it even more, and at this point you hold your breath and think of the last time you tried to pull for a break, and then bend the rod even more. Many times the fish will come away from the snag much more easily than you imagined and in no time at all you're playing it a few yards from the snag but in open water.

The *worst* thing you can do at this stage is to ease off the pressure, maybe even slacken off the drag a notch, because that just gives the fish the freedom and space it needs to wind up enough acceleration to dive back into the snag. It's hard to ignore that feeling of relief when the fish is clear of the snag and apparently not fighting quite so desperately, but *whatever* you do, keep that bend in the rod and get the fish well away from the snag before you begin to ease off at all – and even then be very wary of them making a sudden and determined attempt to have another go.

Stalking and snag fishing can be the most exciting of all forms of carp fishing, providing you go about it with the right gear and with confidence. Without either of those – don't bother! And don't bother if the odds of the fish escaping are too much on the fish's side.

15 BECOMING A SMARTER CARPER

What is fishing, really? It's a peculiar pursuit of happiness, or at least it seems a strange way to find enjoyment if you're one of those unfortunate people who have never been 'hooked' on angling. The path we follow is usually along the lines of giving fishing a try with a friend or two, finding we enjoy it, and then taking it a lot more seriously as we decide to make it a regular leisure pursuit. At this stage most of us are fishing for more or less anything, anywhere. Only later in our angling careers do some of us decide to specialize in hunting bigger fish, and then many of us narrow this down even further by specializing in hunting a single species, with most of us deciding that carp offer us all we want from angling.

We continue to strive to improve our fishing skills by reading as much as we can, watching angling DVDs, and noting what other successful anglers are doing whilst we fish the same waters. This chapter in our angling career, if we remain keen anglers, lasts for the rest of our lives, for we never stop learning. There is always something, some little scrap of knowledge that another angler has that has never occurred to you. Likewise, you will know something advantageous that he doesn't.

The most unfortunate anglers are those who think they know it all, who have fished for a number of years and come to believe that they have nothing else to learn. What they don't realize is that we will *never* know it all, and the constant striving for more knowledge is a major part of the enjoyment we derive from angling. Solving the puzzles that fish – carp, in our case – set us, is the 'kick' that we get from it, and seeing a change in method or bait outsmart a big carp is one of the most thrilling experiences on the planet the moment it slides over the net. It's a wonderful feeling knowing that a plan has worked.

The constant search for knowledge, the learning and striving to outwit crafty carp is the path

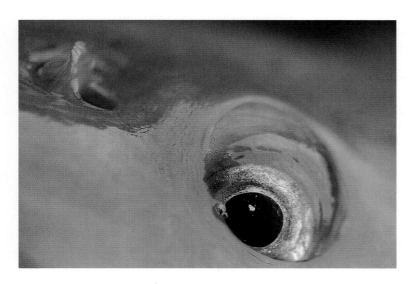

Smell and sight – just two of the carp senses you'll have to fool if you want to catch a big carp.

When you're this close to a big carp you realize why you do it: the head of a superbly conditioned thirty-pounder (13.6kg).

to angling enjoyment, providing we don't become obsessive to the point where family becomes second best. Such obsession can make you into a secretive and unfriendly angler, the one everyone else avoids and the one who, subsequently, never has the full benefit of any other angler's knowledge. Never lose sight of the fact that we're fishing, and that fishing should be fun and not a race to see who can catch the most and the biggest. Of course there is nothing at all wrong with trying to catch the biggest and the most: just don't allow your efforts to stray into territory that tramples on both good values and friends in the rush to be the best. Make enjoying your fishing your first priority, and doing so without compromising family, friends or anyone else.

So what is the best way to become a smarter carper once you've reached a certain level of competency? The short answer is to keep reading, keep watching the fishing DVDs, and keep listening to other anglers. Carry on experimenting for yourself, trying different methods, different baits and different waters. You'll come to realize that the carp in different waters have subtle and sometimes not-so-subtle differences in behaviour, and that what works on one water could be the kiss of death on another. Don't be afraid to try something that isn't considered

A single day with a top coach such as Ian Gemson should increase your tackle and technical knowledge enormously.

Whether you set your sights high for fish of this size or bigger, or for smaller fare, never lose sight of your angling enjoyment.

conventional in carp angling circles; you may just hit on something that will give you that edge for extracting more carp than is usual from a certain water. It is for that reason that a résumé of float fishing has been included, a method that is not in the typical carp angler's repertoire.

Professional Coaching

If you've reached a certain level in mastering carp fishing but feel that you're not getting something quite right, then it could be a good move to book a day with a qualified angling coach. As with many other sports, there is no substitute for being shown how to do something

by an expert in his field. There are not many qualified professional angling coaches who specialize in teaching how to fish for big carp, but one such coach is Ian Gemson, who is a Level 2, PAA (Professional Anglers Association) coach, who runs Smart Carping (07864 959163, contact@smartcarping.com).

Ian painstakingly explains and demonstrates all the major and finer details to steer you towards becoming a competent carp angler, including how to go about finding features using a marker float, how to feed accurately using a spod, and how to make an effective spod mix, and he ably demonstrates long casting. Furthermore, his lessons on accuracy and demonstrations of how to achieve it are invaluable.

Such hands-on lessons will also give you a feel for the tackle that you may not already own, but which you are thinking about buying. Lessons can also be tailored to your particular requirements, meaning that you can improve an aspect of carping in which you lack expertise, and not waste your time learning about something you're not likely to need.

Although still in its early days with coarse fishing, personal coaching is an excellent way to learn how to fish for carp in the shortest possible time. It is a long-accepted route to competence in most other sports, and indeed with fly fishing. No doubt soon Ian will not be the only one offering professional coaching to specialist carp anglers.

One of the sights that carp fishers see and appreciate: a glorious sunrise.

BIBLIOGRAPHY

There have been many carp books published in the last sixty years. The majority have been instructional, some of which have stood the test of time. Other books trace the history of carp fishing or are simply memoirs, diaries or anecdotal. Some of the books have been compiled with many contributors, and in these cases, only the editor or principal contributor is listed. Although many of the books are still obtainable at a reasonable cost, some older ones are long out of print. The original publisher and date of publication is shown. Modern reprints exist for a number of these, but in some instances, the books are rare, highly sought after and therefore expensive. A search on the Internet should reveal the reprints.

Bailey, John:
Carp – The Quest for the Queen (The Crowood Press, 1986)
Carp Challenge (The Crowood Press, 1994)

Ball, Chris:
The King Carp Waters (The Crowood Press, 1993)
Floater Fishing (Paisley-Wilde, 1991)

'BB':
Confessions of a Carp Fisher (Eyre & Spottiswood, 1950)
Wood Pool (A Carp Water) (Eyre & Spottiswood, 1958)
The Whopper (Eyre & Spottiswood, 1967)

Chillcott, Ian *Tackling Carp with Chilly Chilcott* (Quiller, 2007)

Church, Bob *Big Carp* (The Crowood Press, 2007)

Clifford, Kevin:
Redmire Pool (with Len Arbery) (Beekay, 1984)
A History of Carp Fishing (Sandholme Publishing, 1992)
A Century of Carp Fishing (with Chris Ball and Tim Paisley) (Carptalk Enterprises, 2000)

Crow, Simon *Carp Fishing: Advanced Tactics* (The Crowood Press, 2006)

Crow, Simon and Hughes, Rob:
Strategic Carp Fishing (The Crowood Press, 1997)
Discover Carp Fishing: A Total Guide to Carp Fishing (The Crowood Press, 2002)

Cundiff, Julian *Practical Carp Fishing* (The Crowood Press, 1993)

Gibbinson, Jim:
Carp (Richard Walker Library, 1968)
Big Water Carp (Beekay, 1989)
Carp Sense (Beekay, 1992)
Gravel Pit Carp (Laneman, 1999)

Hearn, Terry *In Pursuit of the Largest* (Bounty-Hunter, 1998)

Hilton, Jack *Quest for Carp* (Pelham Books, 1972)

Hutchinson, Rod:
Rod Hutchinson's Carp Book (Hudson Chadwick Publishing, 1981)
The Carp Strikes Back (Wonderdog, 1983)
Carp, Now and Then (Wonderdog, 1988)

Ingham, Maurice and Rogers, Peter *The Carp Catcher's Club* (Medlar, 1998)

Jackson, Lee *Lee Jackson's Carp Clinic* (EMAP, 2001)

Langridge, John *Aphrodite's Carp* (Medlar, 2006)

Maddocks, Kevin:
Carp Fever (Beekay, 1981)
Carp Rigs (with Julian Cundiff) (Beekay, 1996)

Maylin, Rob:
Tiger Bay (BountyHunter, 1988)
Fox Pool (BountyHunter, 1989)
Carp (Beekay, 1990)
Basil's Bush (BountyHunter, 1993)

Miles, Tony:
Carp Fishing (The Crowood Press, 1991)
The Carp Years (Little Egret, 2006)

Mohan, Peter *Basic Carp Fishing* (Beekay, 1982)

Paisley, Tim:
Carp Fishing (The Crowood Press, 1988)
Carp Baits Uncovered (Angling Publications, 1991)
Tales from the Bivvy (Angling Publications, 1994)
To Catch a Carp (The Crowood Press, 1997)
Carp! (Angling Books, 2002)

Sharman, George *Carp and the Carp Angler* (Stanley Paul, 1980)

Various *For the Love of Carp* (The Carp Society, 1989)

Walker, Dick *Stillwater Angling* (Macgibbon & Kee, 1953)

Wilson, John *Catch Carp* (Boxtree, 1991)

Yates, Chris:
Casting at the Sun (Pelham Books, 1986)
The Secret Carp (Merlin Unwin, 1992)
Four Seasons (Medlar, 1996)

INDEX

angling travel agents 166

back leads 116
bait:
  bands 86
  boats 142
  delivery gear 83–6
  drills 86
  float fishing 177
  surface fishing 152
baits:
  artificial 62
  attaching to hook 101
  boilies 59–62
  boilies, air-dried 61–2
  bread 49, 56, 153
  casters 55
  Chum Mixer 153
  colours 62
  dog biscuits 153
  flavours 53–4
  hemp 56
  magic 51
  maggots 54–5
  method groundbait 110–14
  paste 59–60
  pellets 57–9, 114
  pop-ups 153
  seeds 56–7
  spod mix 62–4
  sweetcorn 56
  traditional 54
  worms 55–6, 154
baiting campaigns 162
baiting needles 86
bank sticks 90
barrows 91
bedchairs 83
best swims 36–7
bite:
  alarms 88–9
  detection 87–9
  bites 117
bivvy 81–3
  accessories 83
  domes 82–3
  shelter 82
boats, rowing 141, 165
bobbins 117
bolt rig 98, 104
braid stripper, Korda 87
bubblers 36–7
butt grips 90

cameras 92
Canada 165
Cardus, Eddie 19
carp care 92, 131–2
carp waters 12–13, 31–6
carp, common 23
  crucian 22
  grass 22
  growth rates 26
  habits 24–31
  intelligence 24
  koi 24
  longevity 26
  mirror 23
  varieties 22–4
casting, technique 135, 137
catapults 84–5
chairs 83
channels 44
chod rig 107
club waters 13
coaching 186–7
confidence rig 107
controllers 152, 154
cooking equipment 92

disgorgers 79

feature finding 47–8
features, water 41–7
feeding triggers 30–1
finding fish 36–7
fisheries, commercial 12
fishing abroad 164–6
float fishing 173–80
   feeding 179
   tackle 174–6
   tactics 179
   waters 174
floats and controllers 152
forceps 79, 80
France 165
freelining 154

Gemson, Ian 186
gravel bars 32
gravel pits 32
gripper lead 48
groundbait 62–3
   method 110–14

hair rig 98, 101, 103
hangers 87
Harrison, Dr Stephen 69–70
head torches 91
heavy metal putty 60, 107
helicopter rig 105
hiding the line 114–15
holdalls 90–1
hook sharpener 94
hookbait mounting tackle 86
hooks 93–4, 151, 176
   choosing 94
   Korum Seamless 93
   surface fishing 151
hooklinks 99–101, 109
   braided 99–100
   length 101
   monofilaments 100
   stiff 101
   surface fishing 151–2
hot-spots 40

in-line leads 95

keep sacks 80–1
Klin-Ik, Kryston 79
knot puller, Korda 87

knots 103
   knotless 99–100
   Mahin 76

landing carp 127–9
landing nets 77
leaders, fluorocarbon 115
lead core 95–6, 115, 117
leads, back 116
   casting 95
   dumpy 95
   gripper 48
   in-line 95
line aligner 103
lines 74–6
   braided 75, 99, 151
   fluorocarbon 75–6, 115
   monofilament 74–5, 175
   shock leaders 76
   surface fishing 151
long-range fishing 133–48
   accuracy 134, 137–41
   boats and bait boats 141–2
   feeding 135, 141
   realistic casting distance 135
   rods and reels 137
   spodding 148
long session fishing 16, 159–64
   baiting campaign 162
   camping out 160–2
   stay put or move 163–4
   supplies and hygiene 162
luggage 90–1

maggot klip, Korda 55
mapping a water 46
margin fishing 178
margins 44–6
marker floats 47
method fishing 109–14
   hook link 109
   hookbait 109–10
   how it works 110–11
   mix 111–14

organization 121–2

playing carp 122–7
   on a short line 179–80
prebaiting 162

preoccupied feeding 50–1
preparation 121
problems perceived 119–20
purpose-built waters 34–5
putty 60, 107
PVA 142
  bags 143–4
  bait sticks 144–5
  dissolving or pop-up foam 144
  string and tape 143

quick-release leads 104

record, Chris Yates 26
record, world common 21
Redmire Pool 17
reels 72–4
  Baitrunner 72
  big pit 73–4, 137
  centre-pin 74, 175
  fixed-spool 72, 74, 151, 175
  free spool/bait-runner type 72
  surface fishing 151
rigs 96–108
  advanced 105–8
  basics 97, 103–5
  bolt 98–9, 104
  chod 107
  confidence 107
  creating 86–7
  hair 98
  helicopter 105–7
  in-line 104–5
  line aligner 103
  pendulum 105
  running 104–5
  semi-fixed 104–5
  storing 86–7
  understanding and developing 97–8
  weed or rotten bottom 108
rod:
  handles 70–1
  holdalls 90
  pods 89
  rings 70–1
rods 66–71
  how many 120
  actions 66–72
  barbel 72, 174
  long casting 69, 137

spodding 72
surface fishing 150
test-curve 68–70
rucksacks 90
running rig 104–5
runs 117

sacks 80
scales 79–80
shelter 81
shock leaders 76
slack lining 116–17
snag fishing 181–3
  playing technique 181–3
  tackle 181
spodding 145–8
spods 147–8
spod mixes 62–4
springers 87
stalking 11, 156–7, 180–1
  gear 180
surface fishing 149–58
  baits 152–4
  methods 154–8
  tackle 150–2
swingers 87
swivels 96

temperature 28–30
Terminator, Daiwa 69
throwing sticks 85–6
torches 91

unhooking mats 77–8

weed 42–3
weed rig 108
weigh slings 79
weights 94–5
winter carping 167–72
  baits 172
  choosing a water 170
  keeping warm 168–70
  locating the fish 170
  tackle and tactics 170–2

Yates, Chris 26

zig rig 155